Restore My Glory
A Glow Up Guide & Stories of Restoration

By Chiamaka Gulley

Restore My Glory
Copyright © 2024 By Chiamaka Gulley
A product of Gulley Generations

All rights reserved. This book or any portion thereof may not be reproduced or used in any manner whatsoever without the express written permission of the author except for the use of brief quotations in a book review.

All scriptural references are from the King James Version of the Holy Bible.

This book is for every girl and woman. The one who is going through or has overcome a battle. To the young girls that need guidance and hope through this journey we call life. You matter and you are stronger than you can imagine. Little sisters, big sisters, aunties, and grandmas also. To all our beautiful daughters, this is for you. Learn from our stories and mistakes, may you be the absolute best version of us. Be blessed and encouraged in your generation. Stand tall and firm because the battle you face has a purpose.

Foreword by Shari Stephens

This collection of real-life, overcoming testimonies will change your life and point you in the direction of Jesus for healing, deliverance, freedom, and joy!

There is nothing more powerful than real life experience. You can't deny the impact of what someone has gone through and endured. Restore My Glory is a collection of powerful testimonies from ladies with vastly different life experiences. They all share one common thread, each faced devastation, pain, and hurt. In their trials they called out to God and found healing, answers, and restoration through Him.

Women in general have a very tough road to travel. Whether it's through the sexualization of our young girls or the different trials experienced though womanhood. There are battles every female will face throughout their lives. Restore My Glory seeks to let you know that you can make it.

In this book you will not only learn from others triumph through their adversity but gain wisdom, guidance, and encouragement so that you may avoid them entirely. This book is a plea, a cry out to our little sisters and women throughout the world to say, we made it through by the grace of God and so can you. His healing and restorative power is there if you need it. Wisdom is also there to keep you if you choose it.

If you are dealing with the pain of molestation, loss of a child, loneliness or confusion over your sexual orientation, this book will share a journey to wholeness shared by a real-life woman who made it through and is still standing. Maybe you just don't fit in, you're a stranger in a new land, or you need a friend. These prevailing women will help to shed light on your path. These devastating life challenges are designed to destroy you, but God has purposed to make you whole and restore your glory. Just as these women have remained standing, you can too. There is so much ahead of you dear sister, and it is our prayer that any of the struggles and testimonies that they have experienced will result in your deliverance, making your story a testimony for someone else.

And they overcame him by the blood of the Lamb, and by the word of their testimony. Revelation 12:11

Get ready for the healing and the truth that you are not alone. The trials you face are common, but these ladies have stood through them and offer proof that you too can survive and thrive by God's grace.

Contents

Introduction

Chapter One - Identity Crisis
Bridget's Testimony A Leap of Faith

Chapter Two - The Glow Up
Joana's Testimony As A Child

Chapter Three - You are Beautiful
Amarachi's Testimony Only One

Chapter Four - Time is Precious
Shadia's Testimony Teen Mom

Chapter Five - Build Your Legacy
Sasha's Testimony To My Baby

Chapter Six - Influence
Janique's Testimony Plan B

Chapter Seven - Speak Life
Chibudom's Testimony Waiting

Chapter Eight - New Beginnings

Introduction

The foundation of a home is the most important part. The purpose of a foundation is to create stability and durability. It plays a pivotal role in the longevity of a home. Women we are the builders of our homes, figuratively speaking. Architecture is necessary but environment is crucial.

A firm foundation is a must. Build on a foundation that can withstand floods, disasters and structural calamity. Every detail of our homes, makes an impact. The atmosphere and pace we create, sets the tone. There are many seasons that come and go. In life there will always be spring, summer, fall and winter. Over time with wear and tear, just like any home, renovation and restoration become a necessity. The condition of our homes often need some love and care.

The dictionary definition of the word "restore" is, to bring back to or put back into a former or original state.

If you find that your foundation is broken and torn apart, restoration is possible at any given moment. A firm foundation is vital to growth and success. I subscribe to you that the secret to truly glowing up is to heal your inner wounds while taking accountability for who you are and are becoming. It matters how we speak, what we listen to, and the friends we keep. Women we have an unhealthy obsession with beautifying our outer self, while our inner self is neglected. When your inner person shines it will trickle to the outward. Small changes every day will help bring us closer to the image we aspire to be.

I have read a lot of self help books and worked so hard on trying to change myself. My efforts were futile. I neglected to realize that real change starts with transformation. I needed to heal my mind, body and soul from the bad decisions that I made. I finally took accountability and acknowledged that I could make transformative changes with how I thought. Our thoughts shape the foundation of our lives. Before setting plans into motion, it all begins with a single thought. If you are looking for a way to truly glow up, this guide is for you. Let's learn from each mistake and make a genuine effort to grow from within. The real "glow up" is wisdom. Wisdom is priceless.

There will be practical solutions and engaging stories that will hopefully help you overcome the trials you face. Be prepared to be encouraged, challenged and uplifted. There will be Scripture Meditation, Things to Ponder and Prayer. At the end of each chapter you will read various testimonies of women who just like you were faced with the impossible. These stories are powerful and display the glory of God. You will have the opportunity to be still, and hopefully find clarity in the season of life you find yourself in. Try your best to be honest and apply yourself.

The Goal

By the end of this book, my dream is for you to have the tools to rebuild and restore your foundation, no matter the current condition. This book is a result of obedience and faith. I had no desire to ever write a book but I hope that my obedience helps a girl, or woman that might need this. I want you to find yourself in this book, and grow from everything you have been through and are going through. We all have a story to tell and yours might help the next girl persevere. You got this sister, I know you can do this! My inspiration for this book comes from a Proverb.

> *Every wise woman buildeth her house: but the foolish plucketh it down with her hands. Proverbs 14:1*

Scripture Meditation

Psalm 11:3
If the foundations be destroyed, what can the righteous do?

Proverbs 2:6
For the Lord giveth wisdom: out of his mouth cometh knowledge and understanding.

Proverbs 3:13-18
Happy is the man that findeth wisdom, and the man that getteth understanding. For the merchandise of it is better than the merchandise of silver, and the gain thereof than fine gold. She is more precious than rubies: and all the things thou canst desire are not to be compared unto her. Length of days is in her right hand; and in her left hand riches and honour. Her ways are ways of pleasantness, and all her paths are peace. She is a tree of life to them that lay hold upon her: and happy is every one that retaineth her.

Proverbs 8:11
For wisdom is better than rubies; and all the things that may be desired are not to be compared to it.

Matthew 7:24-27
Therefore whosoever heareth these sayings of mine, and doeth them, I will liken him unto a wise man, which built his house upon a rock: And the rain descended, and the floods came, and the winds blew, and beat upon that house; and it fell not: for it was founded upon a rock. And every one that heareth these sayings of mine, and doeth them not, shall be likened unto a foolish man,

which built his house upon the sand: And the rain descended, and the floods came, and the winds blew, and beat upon that house; and it fell: and great was the fall of it.

Ephesians 2:20-22
And are built upon the foundation of the apostles and prophets, Jesus Christ himself being the chief corner stone; In whom all the building fitly framed together groweth unto a holy temple in the Lord: In whom ye also are builded together for an habitation of God through the Spirit.

James 1:5
If any of you lack wisdom, let him ask of God, that giveth to all men liberally, and upbraideth not; and it shall be given him.

Proverbs 3:7
Be not wise in thine own eyes: fear the LORD, and depart from evil.

Proverbs 4:7
Wisdom is the principal thing; therefore get wisdom: and with all thy getting get understanding.

Proverbs 9:10
The fear of the LORD is the beginning of wisdom: and the knowledge of the holy is understanding.

1 Corinthians 1:30
But of him are ye in Christ Jesus, who of God is made unto us wisdom, and righteousness, and sanctification, and redemption:

Things To Ponder

What part of my foundation is broken? (Marriage, mind, body, heart etc.)

What areas of my life need restoration?

What holds me together when my life has storms?

What path do I envision for my life?

Do I focus more on my inner or outer beauty?

What principles do I build my life on?

What does the restored me look like?

Prayer

Lord I pray for wisdom, and grace to understand your heart for my life. Please direct my steps and fill me with your truth. Heavenly Father please heal my foundation. If there are any cracks, insecurities or damage please restore those areas of my life.

Open my heart to your Word and Truth. The truth will set me free, so please prepare my heart and mind to receive what you have in store for me. Give me eyes to see, and ears to hear what the Spirit is saying. Heal me Lord, I need you. In Jesus name. Amen!

Chapter One
Identity Crisis

Shari is my mother in law. I am so grateful for the example of Christ she models daily. You have been instrumental and supportive from the day we met. Thank you for helping raise the best man I have ever known.

Yolo

Most of us think for the here and now. We all know the term 'yolo' (you only live once). I implore you, as the builder of your home to think beyond today. Think about the generations to come and the impact that we will have on them. It is clear that our society is broken and hurting. The reason most of us are trapped in destructive patterns, is due to them being passed on to us. We can change that narrative and strive to be greater.

Our children and the next generation depends on it. Generational patterns of destruction ends with you. Declare that over your life. Remember thoughts are the building blocks. Our thoughts drive our habits and behaviors. I have challenged every thought pattern by thinking beyond my circumstances.

For example, When I met my mother in law for the first time she looked at me and said "I prayed for you from the moment I had my son." What a powerful statement. It blew me away and gave me chills! With tears in my eyes I was truly humbled. A woman I had never met, prayed for me from the day she had her son. Think about that and how powerful that is. I now do the same over my children because she passed on that wisdom. I was accepted with open arms and loved by her. The mother in law, and daughter in law rivalry is nonexistent between us. We build and love each other. Sisters what we do now matters, it will echo and effect the next generation.

The decisions we make and how we live our lives, all matters. The way we speak to our children will build or tear them down. The point is we all started as children. What we experience as children can affect our entire lives. Some of you have been abandoned, neglected, abused, raped, and you might even be an orphan. If that is you please continue reading. You are loved and seen. Hopefully by the end of this book you are filled with hope.

Throughout my life I have been blessed with wonderful examples of women in my life. I know that might not be the case for some of you reading this. Take heart, there is hope in every season of life that we journey through. There will be moments when we are sad, discouraged and hopeless. The most important thing is not to stay in those emotions but to continue looking ahead.

Your generation to come and your path towards healing matter. Your story might be the very thing another girl hears, and feels understood for the first time. The pain and failures of this life allows us to encounter our reality. We are frail and human.

It is important to find a tribe that can help pray and uplift the burdens we face. Women we need each other now more than ever before. When we release jealousy, hatred and comparison we are so much better together. I have had my fair share of burdens that I have borne. And it all started as a little girl. I faced an identity crisis.

Tomboy

I grew up with what I thought was a boyish figure. I was very thin, no hips, breasts, or anything that seemed 'womanly'. I grew up in a culture that glorified curvacious women. The bigger the better, being thin was frowned upon. My disappointment only grew when puberty came and went without any bodily change. I started wearing baggy shirts and pants in an effort to hide my lanky figure. At a point I would wear two to three pairs of pants to create the illusion of being bigger than I was. With time I started to become more athletic and really started looking and feeling more boyish, so I thought.

Reluctantly, I embraced being a tomboy. I mowed lawns, had a newspaper route, and enjoyed tag football with the boys at school. In addition, family friends began calling me tomboy also. I started to believe that maybe I was meant to live out that role. It felt natural. In addition, I did not receive many compliments growing up.

Fortunately, I did not stay in this identity. I always knew I was more than just a tomboy. Thankfully with time I learned how to do laundry, sew, clean and cook with my mom. During this time I was entrusted with the care of children. Being a baby sittter brought me immense joy. One day becoming a mother was always a dream of mine. In life there are many different roles we play as women. Maturing in the new seasons of life requires flexibility.

Attention

A new season came to pass. My family moved cross county to a new city, and there I reclaimed my womanhood and dressed more 'feminine'. It was a fresh start and I took the opportunity to shed my tomboy identity. I was relieved to start over and be a new person. It was nice not to have the neighborhood looking at me, as just the tomboy. It was exciting to be viewed as a woman finally, and I gave this new season my very best shot!

I got a new wardrobe, and started wearing very tight clothing to prove and display the curves I had attained as a teenager. With this reclamation came the hunger for attention. I was determined to be attractive, and beautiful. I finally got attention and compliments but not from the right sources. It came from people that wanted to take advantage of me. This attention was lust and not love. Honestly, ladies it was not worth it. There is more to our bodies than becoming an object of one's affection.

Sadly, it took me years to realize that how I dress matters. If I present myself as a whore, I will get the attention of a whore. If I dress like a lady, I will receive respect as such. I soon realized that the men I attracted had the wrong intentions. The more attention I received the more frustrated I got. Let me explain, my go-to outfit of the day was a crop top and tight yoga pants. Men would stare or say ridiculous things to me. I did not realize that the more I showed, the more derogatory the compliments became. I used to blame men for their lack of will power to not look at my body. I did not want to accept that men are visual but that is a fact.

How we dress will always be the first thing people notice, because it is visible. The core issue was that I wanted attention, but when I got it, I then blamed men for lusting after me. Truly, if I wanted respect, I had to start dressing with dignity. My motivation was flawed. And after years of harassment, I needed a change.

I encourage you to look within and ask if what you are wearing is pleasing to God or to a man? Think about it, when was the last time you saw a Queen or Princess dressed inappropriately? It rarely happens because they know their position. We love to call ourselves queens and princesses, but the way we dress is a different story. Knowing and playing your position is powerful. Girls, I can tell you from experience, any man that wants you just for your body is not a good option. When you are presenting yourself in public and choosing a husband, it is wise to choose a man that is not lustful.

This is where generational thinking and planning are important. Character matters and the very man you attract will either be your dream man or a nightmare. Pause and please meditate on that. This is not just based on appearances but also a mindset of purity. There are women who dress modestly but have filthy hearts. This is a heart issue not just based on appearance.

Although purity is scarce in our society, it is a precious commodity, and it matters. I wish I had known this at a younger age. I wore things that were degrading to myself and brought the wrong attention. The root cause was my lack of fatherly love and attention.

The Root

My father passed away when I was eight years old. Being that young I did not fully understand nor was I aware of the impact of his death. I have no memories of my dad that I can recall even now. Looking back, the pain was so deep that I just numbed and blocked it.

Growing up I did not get to hear often that I was beautiful. I longed and craved attention because of that loss. My dad was not there to affirm or tell me the things a girl so desperately must hear from a father figure. I did not realize that my poor decisions of dressing immodestly and seeking validation from male attention stemmed from this void. Sadly, not having a physical father brought years of pain and heartache to me.

If you have a similar background or an absent father or mother, may God comfort and restore you. I know that pain and constant longing for approval. Just know that you have a Heavenly Father, and you are a daughter of King Jesus. If this is your first-time hearing this, know that it is true. You are loved and He is a good Father and created you just the way you are and wants to restore you. The Father to the fatherless.

To God be the glory I am now walking in a new light and identity. It has been a long journey, but the Lord thankfully is in the restoration business. He is a restorer, and I am a testimony of his love and grace! I now dress with the right intention. I want to present myself as the daughter of a King. I am not perfect and still learning what that looks like. Since changing my style of dressing, respect has followed. To my surprise, there have not been any derogatory comments, at all.

Solution

I implore you sister to adorn yourself accordingly, as a child of a KING. I am not here to tell you that it is only skirts or dresses. I am here to encourage you to dress with the right motive. You are not accountable to me and have the freedom to dress how you want. It has been a process for me and did not happen overnight, I had to relearn how to present myself and I am still learning. Girls, I have been in your shoes and have worn skintight skirts, yoga pants, and dressed immodestly. It is not worth it. I still regret the men I have caused to stumble by the way I used to dress.

If you are seeking a respectable man, you must be respectable in your appearance to attract him. For example, when we apply for a job, we dress with success in mind for the interview. The same should apply when presenting for a potential husband. If lust attracts him, you will have to maintain that to keep him, and that is exhausting trust me. The next girl that barely has clothes on, he might fall for.

Simply put, dressing scantily and immodestly attracts predators. We should not wonder why both men and women have lost respect for one another. We have objectified each other, and it is destroying our society. If we reclaim respect for ourselves and conduct ourselves with class, we will then regain our dignity.

Be wise and learn from my mistakes. The way you dress matters for generations to come. The choice is yours depending on how you present yourself. A little girl is watching and will emulate the way you dress one day. Look in the mirror and before leaving home, simply ask yourself. What kind of attention or man will I attract with my attire?

Scripture Meditation

Father To the Fatherless

Exodus 22:22
Ye shall not afflict any widow, or fatherless child.

Deuteronomy 10:18
He doth execute the judgement of the fatherless and widow, and loveth the stranger, in giving him food and raiment.

Psalm 68:5
A father of the fatherless, and a judge of the widows, is God in his holy habitation.

Job 29:12
Because I delivered the poor that cried, and the fatherless, and him that had none to help him.

Zechariah 7:10
And oppress not the widow, nor the fatherless, the stranger, nor the poor; and let none of you imagine evil against his brother in your heart.

2 Corinthians 6:18
And will be a Father unto you, and ye shall be my sons and daughters, saith the Lord Almighty.

James 1:27
Pure religion and undefiled before God and the Father is this, To visit the fatherless and widows in their affliction, and to keep himself unspotted from the world.

Modesty

1 Peter 3:3-4
Whose adorning let it not be that outward adorning of plaiting the hair, and of wearing of gold, or of putting on of apparel; But let it be the hidden man of the heart, in that which is not corruptible, even the ornament of a meek and quiet spirit, which is in the sight of God of great price.

Proverbs 31:25-30
Strength and honour are her clothing; and she shall rejoice in time to come. She openeth her mouth with wisdom; and in her tongue is the law of kindness. She looketh well to the ways of her household, and eateth not the bread of idleness. Her children arise up, and call her blessed; her husband also, and he praiseth her. Many daughters have done virtuously, but thou excellest them all. Favour is deceitful, and beauty is vain: but a woman that feareth the Lord, she shall be praised.

1 Timothy 2:9-10
In like manner also, that women adorn themselves in modest apparel, with shamefacedness and sobriety; not with broided hair, or gold, or pearls, or costly array; But (which becometh women professing godliness) with good works.

Proverbs 7:10
And, behold, there met him a woman with the attire of an harlot, and subtil of heart.

Proverbs 6:25
Lust not after her beauty in thine heart; neither let her take thee with her eyelids.

Things To Ponder

What legacy will I leave for my family, children, and this world?

What generational patterns are in my family (Addiction, mental illness, poverty, abuse etc.?

Do I compare myself to others?

Have you ever faced an identity crisis?

Who did I learn how to dress myself from?

What kind of man will I attract with the way I currently dress?

Who am I and what is my identity?

Prayer

Father thank you for loving me. Help me to know that I am your daughter and accepted and loved by you. Jesus died for all my sins and saved me through His blood. Father, please heal my heart of all the things I have done that have not brought you joy or glory.

I ask for your forgiveness for the ways that I have dressed and behaved contrary to your word of being modest. Help me to dress with the right intention. Please deliver me from the despair and consequences of my bad decisions. Heal me of any abuse, rape, injustice, or anything that was out of my control.

Lord, please help me to see myself the way you see me. In my brokenness you still see me as whole. Open my eyes to see that you are my Father and care for me. In Jesus name. Amen!

Bridget's Testimony

Leap of Faith

My story begins in the Northern part of Nigeria named Zaria. My dad was in the Nigerian army at that time. We were stationed in Lagos, where I got my primary and secondary education. My parents were originally from a town called Egbema, a very remote area of eastern Nigeria.

When I was growing up people did not believe that women should pursue education, but my father thought different. Unfortunately, during this time, the Nigerian Civil war broke out when I was ten. My dad was now in the Navy. During this time of war, for three years we were separated from my dad.

We returned to the village, due to uncertainty of the outcome of the war. During this time, we had to fend for ourselves because there were no resources coming for us. We farmed, hunted and we fished for our food. It was an exceedingly challenging time. To add, we had no idea whether my dad was alive or dead, communication was nonexistent.

We heard rumors about him being killed, and he apparently heard the same about us. We dodged and survived bombs and bullets. Present danger was near us constantly. There was starvation all around us and children were dying of severe malnutrition, known as kwashiorkor.

At the end of the war in 1970, my dad sent an uncle to check to see if we were still alive. When my uncle discovered we were alive, he reunited us to our dad. I must add that during the war my father thought we were dead and married two wives. I am the first born of twelve children, through polygamy.

My mom was his first wife and miscarried four children in total. She had my sister and me. Subsequently he married a few wives to have male children. My dad in all honesty succumbed to societal pressure to have male offspring. It was a different time then.

My Dream Man

At this point I lost three years of school. When we returned to Lagos, I resumed school and was able to catch up with my age group. Thankfully, I graduated high school with my class. At this time, my dad had retired from the Navy and went back home to the village to live. I attended college in the East and became the first woman to graduate in our whole community and family. I also was valedictorian of my college.

After graduation from college, I met the man of my dreams. We were childhood playmates and reunited after college. He proposed to me on the night of my graduation party, we married a year later. We started having children immediately, and ended up with six children by the time I knew it. After the third child I got saved and became a born-again believer. Furthermore, at this point I began my career as a Nurse Midwife in Owerri. I was working full time and raising my children.

One day I was admitted to the hospital for surgery. While there I learned about a test called CGFNS from a nurse preparing for this test. This test is a proficiency test of English and Nursing practice. An opportunity to travel abroad to America was the last thing on my mind, but when I heard about this test and the details I was interested.

Let me add that my fourth child was born with a congenital abnormality. She was born with a condition called microtia (missing/malformation of an ear). I had been to many doctors and consultants to no avail. They all told me that I needed to travel abroad to receive the kind of help I was looking for. My interest was piqued when this fellow nurse told me about this test.

Greener Pastures

The process began, I ordered the books from the US along with the study guide. And in the process of all this planning I got pregnant again! Did I forget to mention that this test was only available in Ghana, so I traveled eight months pregnant to Ghana to take this test. To God be the glory I passed, on my first try.

I was able to find an agent that visited Nigeria to recruit nurses. Travelling while pregnant was ill advised and I had to wait until after the baby's arrival to travel to the US. At this time, my travel documents were all set, but I could not travel.

Three months after my baby's arrival I left for the US, In June of 1993, in search of greener pastures. I left behind a three-month-old baby, five other children, and my husband. That was an exceptionally long flight. Leaving my family was the most difficult thing I have ever done in my life.

Leaving my baby was a nightmare, I would wake and hear her cry in my dreams. This was a sacrifice, but it was a once in a lifetime opportunity and I knew I had to pursue it. The emotional and physical pain were rough, the abrupt weaning was very painful.

The American Dream

I got to America and lived with my agent and his wife according to the agreement with my husband. The initial period was to take my board exam. I began working as a home health aide and studied tirelessly. Eleven months upon arrival I passed my nursing board exam on my first attempt! They told me it was impossible to pass on the first try, so this was God. After passing the test I secured a job and immediately booked a flight back home to Nigeria to see my family. Prior to this, I filed for a green card.

I spent a year with my family in Nigeria. I traveled back to the US and began filing paperwork for my family to join me. I was working and saving up for a place for all of us to live. At any given point I juggled two to three jobs to achieve this goal. I was focused on reuniting with my family and did whatever it took.

In 1996, my family joined me in Minnesota where I had started. Did I forget to mention that Minnesota has the kindest people in America!? They made me feel so welcome everywhere I went. No surprise we stayed in Minnesota for ten years despite it being the coldest state. We settled, bought a house and were living the American dream. My husband got a job and all the children enrolled in school. Straight away we began my daughter's medical process. We were so happy to be reunited, but it was short-lived.

Nightmare

Tragically, in January 1998 my husband died from an unknown illness. One day he was perfectly fine, the next day we were in the ER and ICU. He died within a week! The autopsy showed it was cancer of the lymphatic system. My youngest at the time was four years old. I was a widow, and had to raise six children alone. To say I was devastated would be an understatement. To add injury to my wound, my husband's family accused me of bringing him to America to kill him. Also, let me mention that I had to send his body back to Nigeria for the burial, again leaving my children.

My church family at the time took turns watching my children during my absence. Culturally speaking sending his body back to Nigeria was mandatory and due to financial straits, I could not afford for my children to accompany me. I am going to pause right here because the unimaginable happened and I could barely breathe let alone think.

After the burial I returned home to take responsibility of raising my six children alone as a single mother. And the rest is history as they say. Or so I thought... In February, the following year in 1999, my father passed away. And I returned to Nigeria again for his burial. My dad's death right after my husband death was tragic and extremely hard on me, I was a daddy's girl. The wounds were reopened. The reality was the two people I loved most were both gone. I cried all the time and felt overwhelmed. It was a nightmare.

Healing

But God, stepped in and helped me through it all. I was on autopilot, and I had to focus all my energy on taking care of my children. My one way of grieving was to remove everything that reminded me of my husband, pictures, and any reminders of him. This was my way of processing my grief. Everyone manages their grief differently. I even moved to another house. It was too much to bear and I needed a new environment after losing him.

I learned to put one foot in front of the other daily and looked up to God every single day. Church and fellowship had a significant impact on getting me through this trial. I surrounded myself with people of faith that spoke life and encouragement into my life daily. The bible became my best friend as a source of strength and encouragement.

I fell into loneliness and thought that finding a man would fill the void my husband had left. I hastily got into a few relationships without thinking it through. I now know that only God can fill these kinds of voids. I learned that the hard way.

Through this experience I often wondered why me? God told me that through this journey I would be able to help others going through widowhood and help them overcome.

I have also forgiven my accusers for the malicious things they said about me when I was going through my trial. Forgiveness is a key element to our faith walk. It is a necessity to forgive those who hurt and slander you. I have found peace in the Lord, and my advice is to trust God. Even when you cannot feel him, or see his hands at work, keep trusting. To the glory of God my children are all alive and well.

I am now a grandmother of thirteen beautiful grandchildren and counting. I wish my late husband could enjoy the grandchildren with me. We spent seventeen years of marriage together and I am grateful for my children and the love we shared. His death impacted all my children differently. My boys went astray but my girls clung to my side and were a source of strength to me. I love you all and did my absolute best. To my future generations always look to God. My favorite scripture that has strengthened me.

> *The LORD is good, a strong hold in the day of trouble; and he knoweth them that trust in him. Nahum 1:7*

Chapter Two
The Glow Up

What a powerful Testimony! I witnessed Bridget's tragedy firsthand. She is my mother. This woman is the reason my faith is unshakable! I am constantly in awe of her strength. She has the biggest heart, and I am blessed that she is my mother.

Failure

Failure happens but do not let it define you. Buckle up ladies, I know failure personally and want to share with you how I overcame it. Examples of my failures include divorce, miscarriage (I do not consider this a failure, but I know the utter feeling of defeat), another identity crisis, hair dye gone wrong with bleach and so much more. I have been through all of this including the hair bleach that made my hair fall out! Do not do it ladies, find a professional! I can laugh about it now. Just know life happens to us all. Do we run and hide or learn to face it head on?

I used to run away from the trials I faced in life. Wherever I ran to, my issues were there waiting for me. In honesty, facing difficulty upset me and caused me discomfort that I did not want to confront. It seemed easier to hide and pretend as if nothing was wrong. I wanted to escape and not face my issues. This coping mechanism did not help to heal the root cause; it just covered it until the scars resurfaced. There were hurts that seemed too deep. Through God's help, one by one I started confronting the inevitable and addressed my problems.

Shattered

When I was twenty-two years old, I was newly married, and pregnant. Things were going well during my pregnancy but suddenly, I went into pre-term labor at twenty-six weeks. I delivered a one pound, one ounce baby girl who then died three days later. My dream in life as I stated before was to be a mother. My life turned upside down, and my heart was shattered. I was downcast and confused. Shortly after losing my child, three months later, I was going through a divorce. This felt like two deaths at once. If you have been divorced, you understand. All my hopes and dreams were gone and mentally I wanted to escape my reality. I cried often, and most nights cried myself to sleep. I honestly felt so broken and without direction.

My faith in God was seriously shaken. I turned to daily marijuana use, and occasionally drank alcohol to mask the pain and the emptiness I felt. I was mourning the death of the dreams I had. Everything was gone overnight. I was in a pit of ruin and despair and did not know where to turn. I found myself angry with God and blamed him for taking my daughter. Often, I struggled with the desire to live. I moved back home for a brief period; I knew isolation would drive me to self-destruction.

I went through years of endless grief and battled with depression and anxiety. I blamed myself also for being the reason my daughter died. If you have lost a child, you understand exactly what I mean by that. The drugs helped numb the pain I felt, and I became dependent on this feeling of not feeling. I ran from the raw emotions that confronted me. I was not ready to address the wound and heal.

Bad Habits

Through marijuana and alcohol, I found myself deeply confused about my sexual orientation. Being a tomboy all those years brought back memories and confused me further. I battled thoughts of homosexuality. Looking back the drugs opened doors of deep darkness and rebellion. I strayed from God and did things my own way during this season. I take accountability and wish that I had coped differently. I paid the consequences for those actions and decisions.

Sin always has a price. Girls, please remember that. Every sin, drug, and door of darkness we open has a price and that price is death. Perhaps not physically but death of the soul. As a backslider I still attended church on occasion during this period. I felt lost but still believed in God. I know it is popular in our culture to mix Jesus with everything, but this is dangerous. I was a hypocrite.

The guilt, shame and the what ifs were so overwhelming. Many of us have found ourselves downcast and have felt abandoned by God. I am here to tell you that He found me, restored me, and renewed me. To God be the glory I am no longer bound by marijuana or alcohol. I am free and the chains of depression and anxiety have been broken. Retelling this story is shameful and brings tears to my eyes. Darkness was all around me but thankfully, the light of God found me.

> Then spake Jesus again unto them, saying, I am the light of the world: he that followeth me shall not walk in darkness, but shall have the light of life. John 8:12

I pray that my vulnerability is helping someone experiencing a tough time after losing their child. Ladies, everything we go through in life can make or break us. I was broken but now I am healed. It was not through my own strength but through the power of the Holy Spirit that I was able to overcome my despair.

My pastor's wife at the time, gave me hope. She too had lost a child and her example of standing firm and strong after her trial encouraged me. God will place you in the right situation at the right time to learn and be encouraged by others.

The Grow Up

One day God allowed me to see that He also suffered a loss of His only begotten Son. He ministered to my heart and told me that He knows exactly what I was going through. He knows our pains and sorrows and is there holding us through the dark nights. With that revelation, know that you do not have to stay in your failure. Life is beautiful and you can dictate a new path. Unfortunately, many of us do not learn from failure.

I implore you to allow failure to grow and mold you into a better person. Look within and be accountable for your own actions. When we fall, it is easy to play the blame game. The best growth in my life has been when I asked myself, what part do I play in all of this? Face your fears, do not allow them to navigate your life.

> *For a just man falleth seven times, and riseth up again: but the wicked shall fall into mischief. Proverbs 24:16*

The world is full of fear and anxieties. Let us be clear, I have fallen prey to both countless times. The fear of the unknown, and thoughts of what if. The thoughts we focus on are seeds, and take root in our hearts. In every season we are like gardens. Sometimes things take time to blossom and grow. Always check your heart for weeds that are overgrown and fruitless.

During this season of loss, I allowed negative thoughts to defeat me. The anxiety I battled started with negative thoughts that would invade my mind constantly. I would get debilitating panic attacks and the spirit of fear would grip and paralyze me. The book of Psalms really helped to calm my mind and navigate the storms of life I faced and still face. Jesus calmed my once anxious mind and heart. It is a battle that continues even after we have overcome it. Stay vigilant and on guard when you have made it to your promised land.

I play the Psalms bible audio most nights as I sleep, to help my thoughts. When we sleep our spirit is still awake, listening to the bible cleanses the soul. Make a habit of listening to God's word day and night. Feed your soul the words of life. It will alter your perception and your discernment will grow.

> So then faith cometh by hearing, and hearing by the word of God. Romans 10:17

I went through my wilderness and am now enjoying the milk and honey that God had in store for me. The trials you face water your beautiful garden of life. Every tear grows and matures you to become the woman God has called you to be. I cried many nights and I remember thinking the pain would never end. The tears are not in vain nor are they wasted. He counts your tears my sister, I really believe that.

Extend grace to yourself and others. We are all growing and learning, so be patient. Everyone's journey of healing from loss is different, some people grieve longer, while others quickly recover. You find what works for you. The important part is to not stay in grief forever, that is not healthy. Seeds take time to grow such as patience, kindness, and temperance. Continue to water your soul with thoughts of peace. Your thoughts are the foundation of your life. Every thought will build or tear down your foundation.

Finding Joy

Here is a nugget of hope. Through all the tragedy and failure, I now have a wonderful husband and two beautiful children. God has turned my mourning into dancing and turned my ashes into beauty.

They that sow in tears shall reap in joy. Psalm 126:5

However, shortly after we got married, I got pregnant, and had a miscarriage (before conceiving my first child). It was very painful and made me question my faith yet again. This time I chose to follow God regardless of my pain and sorrow. He healed my heart and walked me through losing another child. Take heart beautiful sister if this is your story. It is painful and can feel like it makes no sense, but God does have a plan.

Before my second daughter was conceived, God told me to let go of self-hatred. He told me that I was beautiful how He created me and the wigs and fake eyelashes I wore, were not adding to my beauty. I was whole how He made me. I trusted Him, obeyed Him, and threw out my wigs. I wore extensions, and wigs my entire life.

This was a huge deal, and it was rooted in insecurity. This was the first time I embraced my God given hair.

Weeks later I was pregnant. To my amazement I was having a girl as He told me. Twelve years after losing my baby girl, He blessed me with another precious girl. My due date being almost identical. God had me go through that experience for a reason and this time I had to trust him. During the month of my previous daughter's loss, I had great anxiety, but He got me through it and restored my hope and faith. I waited for His perfect timing, and I delivered both of my children with His grace and peace.

My son was my hope and my daughter brought me joy. With each child I have learned so much about myself and my strengths. Women, motherhood is a beautiful thing. May all the mamas going through a loss (still birth, miscarriage, any death, or divorce) be filled with peace and comfort during your trial. For those facing infertility, I pray you find joy in the waiting period. I have experienced both and know how you feel. It is an emotional roller coaster.

Wait on God and His perfect timing He knows how to dry our tears. God has not forgotten about you or about the storm you are facing. Take heart and allow Him to be your rest and anchor during your season of trial and storm. Isolation is not advisable, please seek out the help you may need at this time. Hold on and stay strong. Try to immerse yourself with God's word or in His beautiful creation. Taking a prayer walk, and meditating on the bible can help also.

Scripture Meditation

Psalms 30:11
Thou hast turned for me my mourning into dancing: thou hast put off my sackcloth, and girded me with gladness.

Psalm 34:18-19
The Lord is nigh unto them that are of a broken heart; and saveth such as be of a contrite spirit. Many are the afflictions of the righteous: but the Lord delivereth him out of them all.

Psalm 147:3
He healeth the broken in heart, and bindeth up their wounds.

Romans 5:5
And hope maketh not ashamed; because the love of God is shed abroad in our hearts by the Holy Ghost which is given unto us.

Romans 12:2
And be not conformed to this world: but be ye transformed by the renewing of your mind, that ye may prove what is that good, and acceptable, and perfect, will of God.

Psalm 51:10-12
Create in me a clean heart, O God; and renew a right spirit within me. Cast me not away from thy presence; and take not thy holy spirit from me. Restore unto me the joy of thy salvation; and uphold me with thy free spirit.

2 Corinthians 5:17
Therefore if any man be in Christ, he is a new creature: old things are passed away; behold, all things are become new.

Philippians 4:8
Finally, brethren, whatsoever things are true, whatsoever things are honest, whatsoever things are just, whatsoever things are pure, whatsoever things are lovely, whatsoever things are of good report; if there be any virtue, and if there be any praise, think on these things.

Colossians 3:10
And have put on the new man, which is renewed in knowledge after the image of him that created him:

1 Peter 5:8
Be sober, be vigilant; because your adversary the devil, as a roaring lion, walketh about, seeking whom he may devour:

1 Thessalonians 5:5
Ye are all the children of light, and the children of the day: we are not of the night, nor of darkness.

Hebrews 6:18-19
That by two immutable things, in which it was impossible for God to lie, we might have a strong consolation, who have fled for refuge to lay hold upon the hope set before us: Which hope we have as an anchor of the soul, both sure and stedfast, and which entereth into that within the veil;

Things To Ponder

What dream has died that I really wanted?

What has made me angry with God?

What things have I blamed myself for?

How can I heal and work towards reconnecting with God?

What do I think about all the time?

What am I afraid of?

What things bring me peace?

Prayer

You know me inside and out. Lord I am going through things in my life that need your touch. Please transform me and make me whole. Heal me of all my anxieties and fear. Renew my heart, body, and soul. I give every thought and worry over to you.

Please help me to know that you are my Shepard, and I shall not want. In every valley and situation, you are faithful and my rock. Lead me and guide me into your loving arms. Please help me to overcome intrusive thoughts and negativity in my life.

Father, please break the spirit of addiction from me and my bloodline. Help me to come to a place of being in my right mind. I place my life, my today, and my tomorrows into your hands. In Jesus name. Amen!

Joana's Testimony

As a Child

My first time telling this testimony was in a room full of women. Hundreds if not more. My story is not for me. *"You have to go first to make room for the next person."* This is my testimony, and my goal is to help women find freedom and peace. Sharing our stories always helps someone else.

In 2014, I graduated from high school and that same year, I attended a Dedicated Conference and heard the Lord telling me to move to Las Vegas. What was supposed to be two years, is now going on nine years. I love this house (my church); I love my pastors and I love that I get to be a part of leading people to encounter new life in Jesus. I feel a lot of people know of me, but in reality, a lot of people don't know who I am.

I was born in Chihuahua, Mexico. When I was five or six, we moved to the United States. My parents both worked full-time jobs to provide for us. To which I am extremely grateful for, but unfortunately, that meant they weren't around very much. I am the youngest of four and the only girl (Daddy's girl).

I grew up in a very religious home. No short shorts, no spaghetti strap shirts, only skirts and dresses (which is probably why I don't like wearing them now). Dancing, drinking, tattoos, everything was a sin (whoops). I grew up thinking I had a great life, which I did. But there was a lot I had to go through as a child, and I feel released to share it with you. It is heavy so bear with me...

I was sexually abused starting at the age of five and it continued for years. The few memories I have as a child are those of being sexually abused by my oldest brother. As a child, you don't always know what's right and what's wrong. You allow things because you put your trust in people. You do not know any better. When the abuse finally stopped, I was living my life as one would.

Numb

I could not process what had happened to me or even why, so I tried to numb it out. When I went to middle school, I dated a lot. I created emotional attachments with men to try to fill a void. In high school I began to drink, do drugs, watch pornography and for a moment I even thought I liked women.

You might be wondering how all this happened in a "religious home." Well, my home was strict, my school was not. My parents trusted me and when I wasn't home, I did what I wanted. I was in so much pain and I didn't even know it. I grew up in church and I knew all about a God that loved me, that created me and cared about me, but he was nowhere to be found. I lived my life the way I wanted. I showed up to church every Wednesday and Sunday, but when Monday came around, I was a different person.

In high school, one specific time, I had gone home with a guy I was dating, and I ended up trying to get him off of me. I cried out to God and remember thinking, please get me out of this. By the grace of God, someone walked in, and I was able to push him off and get out of the situation. That was the day I fully dedicated my life to Jesus. That is not what I wanted to do and was not what I wanted to be known for.

Change of Heart

This change of heart wasn't easy at all, my life hit a 360 turn within a matter of a day. My best friends stopped talking to me. People thought I was someone I wasn't, and I was alone. That led me closer to God. During this time God began taking away what I thought I wanted and trading it for what I needed. HIM! Please hear me, I didn't always feel like this. In those moments, I was sad, lonely, and depressed. I didn't understand why things had happened the way they did. My "friends" judged me for sleeping around and took the side of the guy who wanted to take advantage of me.

As I began to have a relationship with God through the remainder of high school, I could not stop thinking about what happened to me as a child. Things began to come to the surface that I didn't know how to deal with.

It started, in my first year of LVBC 2016 (Christian internship at church). The students were invited to sit in a marriage conference session with a well-known pastor. He began to talk about how a lot of married individuals in the room felt misunderstood because they had never talked about the sexual abuse they had encountered at a younger age. He asked them to stand up and my heart dropped. He said there were other people in the room and whether they were married or not, he asked them to stand.

With all the hesitation in the world, I stood up. Tears fell down my face. I felt guilt, shame, and I was embarrassed.

My pastors prayed for me and that was the start of my healing. A respectable pastor's wife slipped me a piece of paper with her phone number on it. I don't remember when or why, but I decided to call her. She invited me to talk, and we sat in her car at a parking lot. She didn't pressure me to talk, we sat there, and I cried. I felt heard for the first time. How beautiful that God always places someone in our life at the right time to help us as we begin our healing journey.

Healing Journey

In November 2017, my brother was in a motorcycle accident. A drunk driver had hit him. Broken bones in his arms, legs, ribs, and his face was unrecognizable. This was the same brother that sexually abused me. Honestly, this was a struggle. I was thankful he was alive, but there was a bitter part of me that wished he had died. Another part of me knew that if he had, I would have never gotten the answers I wanted. I am thankful that during this time I was seeing a counselor to help me.

> *EMDR was also offered (Eye Movement Desensitization & Reprocessing). This method involves moving your eyes in a specific way while you process traumatic memories. EMDR's goal is to help you heal from trauma or other distressing life experiences.*

I spoke with the pastor's wife about how I felt and not a single part of her blamed me or judged me for feeling the way I did, but she didn't let me sit in those thoughts. She allowed me to feel. To this day, I think of how grateful I am because God blessed me with a church family to stand behind me. I never felt alone, I had so many people around me that I could trust.

After my brother's accident, I knew the timing was horrible, but I had to tell my parents. It's now time to tell them everything. On one of my trips to my hometown, to visit my family, I could no longer carry the weight. My dad stayed the night at the hospital, and I decided to tell my mom that night when we got home. After I told her we cried for a few hours. The following morning when my parents traded places, I also told my dad. I had only seen him cry a handful of times, but this news made him cry. I was finally able to breathe and sleep peacefully. More healing began to take place, thank God.

These are some of the steps I took in my journey during my healing process. I read a book called *"Redeeming Love."* I bought it, not knowing what it was about, and it absolutely wrecked me. It was a fictional twist on the Bible story of Gomer and Hosea. The woman in the story had never been taken care of, never been loved, she didn't know who she was, and she didn't think she deserved any of those things. I identified with her. If she cried, I cried. If she was angry, I was angry. That book brought me so much healing.

I also got a counselor. I cried in counseling sessions because I couldn't think of any childhood memories. I felt I had lost an entire part of my life. But consistently going and sharing what I experienced with a professional helped me come out on the other side healed. I was able to share my story and my hurt and they helped me navigate it. I kept godly women around me. I knew they would be able to sit with me, pray for me or even just be in silence. Also reading The Word (bible). I did a lot of devotionals on the Bible app, and the book of 1 Peter helped me.

From 2017 to 2020, I was leading a high school small group and there was a specific girl who had gone through the exact same thing I had. She was a part of the reason why I knew I had to forgive. If I could do it, I knew she would be able to do it too. What was taking me years to process and overcome, I wanted her to do sooner. We sat on the couch one day and with tears in my eyes, I looked at her and said, "I would go through this all over again just so I could sit here with you". I don't know when, but there was a day where all the weight was gone. I knew in my heart that I had made the decision to forgive him, and I did.

I continued to go to counseling, I talked to trusted friends, and I felt good. This was life changing and I was finally free. One day I got a phone call from my other brother. He's panting, unable to catch his breath. He heard a voice saying, "you're going to die today". He called me and I prayed for him. When he calmed down, he began to say, "I'm sorry, I'm sorry". I asked him what he was sorry for, and he said he knew. He knew about the sexual abuse, and he never said a thing. He also felt the weight of what I had carried for years. It wasn't just my story; it was his too. I told him he didn't need to apologize; we were just kids; it wasn't his fault.

This story wasn't just mine. It was his, and it was my parents also. Before I committed to sharing my story, I called my dad and asked him what he thought about me sharing my story. He said, "this is your story, it's important and people need to hear it. Tell the whole world if you must, they need to hear it!"

Restored

I am restored and have found my voice in telling my story. No more shame, guilt, or condemnation. To let you know where I am now, after years of counseling I have forgiven my brother. Since his accident, he couldn't talk, walk, or eat on his own. I used to get mad that I would never get the answers I needed, but I finally feel peace in not knowing.

Sadly, in July 2023 my brother passed away. Choosing to fully forgive him has brought me peace. I share this with you because I know this isn't just my story, this is some of your stories as well and you've never shared it with anyone, or you've never chosen to forgive. I want to encourage you to take the next step! Tell someone! Start the journey of forgiveness. There is a book that says, *"refusing to forgive is refusing the peace of God"*.

You deserve to live in peace, but you must choose to forgive. If my story resonates with you, you are not alone. Statistics say that three out of four women will encounter this at some point in their life. It is not your fault and please don't feel condemned or ashamed.

Find your voice, get your healing, and use your story to help others. Isolation is dangerous after going through this kind of trauma. Please reach out to those you trust and get the help you need. I hope my story can be a steppingstone for you to begin your path of healing. This bible verse is something I hold on to.

> *I will love thee, O LORD, my strength. The LORD is my rock, and my fortress, and my deliverer; my God, my strength, in whom I will trust; my buckler, and the horn of my salvation, and my high tower. I will call upon the LORD, who is worthy to be praised: so shall I be saved from mine enemies. Psalm 18:1-3*

Chapter Three
You are Beautiful

The evening Joana shared her story, I was there in the crowd. Tears rolled down my face endlessly. I was shocked and my heart was broken. I've known her for years and had no idea this was her story. Her spirit is so calm. She has such a purity and peace about her. Ladies, you never know what people are going through on the outside looking in. Thank you for being so brave.

Beauty Standards

Beauty is in the eye of the beholder. You are fearfully and wonderfully made by God. He is the beholder. Take a deep breath. Repeat these words. I am enough. My hair is not a mistake, my lips are by design, my eyes are perfect, and my body is a blessing.

In all of what you think are imperfections, the Lord says you are fearfully and wonderfully made. The devil has sold us lies. We complain and say things like; If only I had those lips, hair, eyes, nose, or body. When we focus on things we do not like, we overlook the things that are blessings.

Waking up each day is a blessing. Having food, shelter and clothing are all blessings we take for granted. I hope these testimonies help you see a different vantage point of life. It is all about perspective. If we frame our mindset properly, the flaws will no longer look like flaws.

In the Old Testament of the bible, after the children of Israel left Egypt, they found themselves in the wilderness. While there, they complained and grumbled about everything! The lord, because of their negative attitude proclaimed they would not enter the promised land. Despite the miracles and wonderful things He had shown them, they focused on the negative. He parted the Red Sea, fed them with manna from the sky and protected them! Joshua and Caleb were the only ones in their generation that entered the promised land. Millions failed to enter due to their heart posture and negative attitude.

Gratitude

God does not take lightly when we speak against how we look because He created us. The next time you feel badly about how you look begin to thank God for the things that are going well in your life. Practicing gratitude matters and will help in restructuring negative thought patterns. The reality is, one day you may have a child and will see yourself in them. For instance, if you take issue with your nose and your child has that same nose, then what? Every detail of your face and body is precious because it is you.

> *Before I formed thee in the belly I knew thee; and before thou camest forth out of the womb I sanctified thee, and I ordained thee a prophet unto the nations. Jeremiah 1:5*

There will never be another human on this earth like you. You are unique and beautiful. The Lord sees you and how precious He made you. He took the time to make every detail of who you are. Just know you are beautiful. There are no exceptions to this truth.

Before my daughter was born, I trashed my wigs and embraced the God given hair on my head. It was more than just my hair though. I had to relearn what beauty is and shed the lies I believed about being beautiful. The truth was I wanted what was not mine. Envy and jealousy are distractions that keep us stagnant.

Look Within

Sadly, our bodies have become a fad. One day being slim is in, then the next day being curvaceous is in. The reality is we want what is not ours. We covet our neighbor's hair, house, car, and body. Remember, the beauty standards we model will be passed on to our children. We must take a moment to think about how we even formed our standards. Who created these standards and what are the implications of adhering to them?

Wherever you go, you take you with you. Joy is not environmental, it is within. No matter where you go, or the surgeries you get to feel beautiful, you are still you. The external might change but the core remains. If you feel inadequate deep inside, making external changes and glowing up might not help. You may still find flaws and the void remains.

Next time you feel unhappy about a feature, start thanking God. When I was younger, I was constantly bullied for having full lips. I hated my lips for years, and now everyone wants lips. Imagine if I changed my lips because of what others said. I grew to love them and be grateful for how I was created.

When I feel critical of myself, I start to thank God for everything I can think of. An external change is a temporary fix. Finding joy is the true key. Beauty is fleeting, we are all aging and growing older. The biggest push in our society for women is "anti-aging." This narrative of not wanting to age is both unrealistic and silly. It is an inevitable fact. We age, and that is okay.

I am intentional during birthdays to find joy in every new year that comes. It is a chance to grow and reflect on areas of life I have matured in. Age well with wisdom rather than just working on your outward beauty. The beauty of this life is in our individuality. If you have modified your body, take heart, God still loves you. The risks of these surgeries are not mentioned enough. There are risks and side effects to any modifications made to the body. Also, it is expensive and at times can be deadly.

Finances

Speaking of finances, we must be wise in our spending. Prior to meeting my husband and getting married, the Lord gave me the task of paying off my debts and instructed me to become debt free. The financial climate is a hot mess we all can agree on. The bills are endless: student loans, car notes, mortgages, beauty maintenance and more. As builders of our homes' finances matter and destructive spending habits can tear down our homes. Did you know that finances are a huge factor in most divorces?

This needs to be addressed. I am not an expert but encourage you to make sure that you are spending from a perspective of building your legacy and family. In the credit card age, we spend what we do not have and create unhealthy habits. Next time you want to buy something new, really ask yourself, is this a need or a want? This question has saved me a lot of money.

My journey to becoming debt free took sacrifice and denial of things I "wanted." For a brief period, I focused on my needs to reach my goals. If this is your goal, it is attainable and requires honesty and sacrifice. When you view things from this angle you realize that most things we purchase are merely wants and not needs.

I challenge you to try it for a month, before buying anything ask yourself that question. We watch other peoples' lives and covet. This is not fruitful and can lead to dissatisfaction. There are ways to help counteract these bad choices. We are lured and influenced through what we see others have. I can testify that I have peace and the trap of comparison is not part of my life. The main reason for this, I believe, is due to not having any social media. It has been about twelve years now.

Social Media

For years I have stayed away from social media and can say that I do not miss it. There was a time I had Myspace and Facebook. Once upon a time on Myspace I had eighty thousand friends! I am not boasting about that and feel foolish for allowing that many people into my life. It got to my head and for my sanity I logged off and never looked back. The comments and pressure to post all the time almost got the best of me. I decided years ago that to live authentically, I could not care what others thought about me. It was very lonely at first, but I soon realized the people that care about me call, text, or meet with me.

Without comparison, I love to see others thriving and enjoying the beautiful things that they have. It is always a temptation to compare myself to others, but I look around and realize that I have everything I need. Sometimes the comparison traps us in an endless cycle of depression and feelings of inadequacy.

'Fomo' is a real thing (feeling of missing out) and it plagues us women differently. Fancy restaurants, travel vlogs, elaborate gender reveals, the list goes on. Most posts are of people living their 'best lives,' and it is easy to mistake it as reality. The allures of online advertisements and Influencers showing the new must haves. Women are bombarded with shiny things daily. Seeing this constantly makes us feel like we need new things. This also proves social media and finances go hand in hand. How many times have you bought something because of social media?

Contentment

Understanding the concept of contentment is a game changer. Before I would make a purchase, I would ask myself if it was a necessity. Usually It was something I saw someone else have. In America, we have a habit of accumulating things with no thought of why we need them. Our garages are filled with random items that collect dust for years. We need to evaluate and put our finances into perspective.

What is your reason and motivation behind your purchases? I am not telling you to stop buying things or to never shop again. However, sometimes these spending habits can sometimes be a band aid over a much bigger issue.

Address the foundation and root causes of what drives you and clarity of mind will hopefully follow. When I became financially free, a burden was lifted off my shoulders. Financial freedom is powerful and can lead to many other blessings.

God made you and you are beautiful. You are one in a billion literally. We have our own unique fingerprint, tongue print, and DNA. No one in the existence of time will ever be you. You are truly one of a kind.

When I removed my wig, I shaved my head and was bald for months. It was liberating and life changing. Please don't shave your head! This was my process and I found freedom. I saved thousands of dollars on not buying wigs. The money we spend to be 'that girl', can be a waste. Especially if we are running from the way God made us. Embrace yourself and see yourself through the lens of God.

Lastly, there are so many women dying unnecessarily through these make over surgeries and augmentations. Keep in mind it all comes with a price. It is a temporary fix to a deeper problem of acceptance. Instead of trying to emulate the next girl, let us applaud the differences that make us all beautiful and unique.

Scripture Meditation

Proverbs 14:30
A sound heart is the life of the flesh: but envy the rottenness of the bones.

Proverbs 22:7
The rich ruleth over the poor, and the borrower is servant to the lender.

Proverbs 27:4
Wrath is cruel, and anger is outrageous; but who is able to stand before envy?

Ecclesiastes 4:4
Again, I considered all travail, and every right work, that for this a man is envied of his neighbour. This is also vanity and vexation of spirit.

1 Peter 5:7
Casting all your care upon him; for he careth for you.

1 Timothy 6:6
But godliness with contentment is great gain.

Philippians 4:11
Not that I speak in respect of want: for I have learned, in whatsoever state I am, therewith to be content.

James 3:16
For where envying and strife is, there is confusion and every evil work.

Luke 12:15
And he said unto them, take heed, and beware of covetousness: for a man's life consisteth not in the abundance of the things which he possesseth.

1 Corinthians 10:31
Whether therefore ye eat, or drink, or whatsoever ye do, do all to the glory of God.

1 Corinthians 10:9-10
Neither let us tempt Christ, as some of them also tempted, and were destroyed of serpents. Neither murmur ye, as some of them also murmured, and were destroyed of the destroyer.

Philippians 2:14-15
Do all things without murmurings and disputings: That ye may be blameless and harmless, the sons of God, without rebuke, in the midst of a crooked and perverse nation, among whom ye shine as lights in the world;

James 5:9
Grudge not one against another, brethren, lest ye be condemned: behold, the judge standeth before the door.

Numbers 14:27
How long shall I bear with this evil congregation, which murmur against me? I have heard the murmurings of the children of Israel, which they murmur against me.

Things To Ponder

When I look in the mirror what do I see?

What masks do I wear to cover what I think are flaws?

Do I have any jealousy or envy toward others?

What is my spending a reflection of?

Am I keeping up appearances or finding contentment in the season I am in?

What are my financial goals?

What different decisions can I make financially that will help me reach my goals?

Prayer

Lord help me to accept your word that says I am fearfully and wonderfully made. Forgive me for wanting to be someone you did not create me to be. Purify my heart and allow me to see myself the way you see me.

Help me to walk in your will for my life and accept the things I hate about myself. You make no mistakes and are working on something beautiful in my life. Thank you for the very breath of life that you have given me on this day.

You are so great and awesome! You created the moon and the stars, yet you chose to create me in your image. Help me to walk in this image of light and of Your glory. And Father God help me to be content in the things that you have blessed me with. I pray for financial wisdom and breakthroughs over my life. In Jesus name. Amen!

Amarachi's Testimony

Only One

My name is Amarachi, which means Grace of God in my native Igbo language. I marvel at the name God gave my mother to name me. It truly has been nothing short of His grace, I stand and share my testimony. I was born in Nigeria, Africa the fourth out of six kids.

I was born with one ear, yes you read that right. When my mom was pregnant with me, she thought she had malaria. She had just ended her birth control and did not think she was pregnant. The morning sickness felt like malaria. Therefore, she proceeded to take medicine while pregnant with me. Spoiler alert, this was not the reason I was born with one ear. Unfortunately, life in Nigeria as a child with birth defects was not ideal. My mom was accused of being a witch because I was "ugly and hideous." She and my father endured the pain and ridicule.

I know most of you are thinking in Nigeria I had no clothes on and was running in a jungle. Believe it or not, we were wealthy. We had hired help such as housekeepers and drivers. We stayed humble and were raised in a Christian home. It was our faith that allowed us to see the good in my defect. I have two brothers and three sisters, and being born with one ear did not change the love they had for me. Surprisingly I was the only one who had a birth defect, my siblings would be what you consider to be "perfect."

In the hopes of migrating our whole family to the United States so we can further investigate my birth defect. My mom after having her sixth child, went to the United States. My mom stayed abroad to prepare the way for us to get a taste of the American dream. Picture this, 1996, at the age of nine, we get some great news that we are moving overseas.

Bullied

We found a prosthetic doctor through our ENT doctor (Ear, nose, and throat), and we were now in the process of getting insurance to approve it. Sadly, Insurance denied the plea for me to receive this life changing ear. They called it plastic surgery. I was devastated, but my mom is a fighter! She was a nurse and had the drive to fight for my cause. She pleaded with the state of Minnesota (the Governor), to see that this was not plastic surgery but a necessity.

At this point a prosthetic ear would make life a little easier for me. During this time, I was in middle school. The bullying and attacks were getting so bad. Honestly, those days were depressing and unbearable. You would not believe the amount of backlash and bullying I received for a condition that I had no say or control over. This was not my choice or any fault of mine; it occurred while I was in the womb. I was called names such as one ear monkey, and African booty scratcher. It was miserable and I vividly remember one day at school a young man brought a gun, to shoot me because I was so "ugly." This was a very scary experience to say the least.

Luckily, they finally accepted the notion for the ear to be covered by insurance. Getting a prosthetic ear would help me a great deal. My school days still consisted of me coming home every day from school crying myself to sleep. I would just sit and think of all the names people called me and just how awful I was treated. All because I did not look like the next average Jane.

I was so grateful for my older siblings (my two brothers and sister). They constantly risked it all at my expense to silence all the hate that came my way. To this day I am forever grateful for all they did for me. My mom constantly encouraged me to pray for those who hated me. That was not easy for me to do as a young girl, but I now see that it was for the best. It took years for me to heal from those painful labels.

Daisy

Fast forward, we moved to a new city. I finally got a chance to meet new people. I had my prosthetic ear that covered my missing ear. I was no longer getting teased because most people did not know about my condition. Years later I met my husband, and it was love at first sight! I have been happily married for almost nine years and we have gotten this far only by God's grace.

In this season of life, the biggest test of my faith was the loss of our sweet baby girl, Daisy Amara. I got married in November 2015. A month after the wedding, my OBGYN told me, I have a cancerous fibroid. The only way to save me was to remove my left ovary and tube. I agreed because in my mind that was the only way. I had surgery in February 2016, and they checked the fibroids, it was not cancerous! I was grateful for that report but bummed at the idea of only having one ovary, especially with my desire to have a big family.

Fast forward to November 2017, I found out I was finally pregnant. We were so excited, we announced it to the world! We did a gender reveal on my birthday in March, and we found out it was a baby girl! God answered our prayer. Pregnancy was smooth sailing. We enjoyed our baby shower, and the baby's room had a beautiful daisy lamp in place, with a furry chic white area rug. We were just in the waiting and anticipating stage. March 24, I graduated with my bachelor's degree carrying Daisy in my womb.

There were so many new adventures that had taken place. July 12th my bestie goes into labor and her sweet baby girl comes around midnight on Friday July 13th. The best part is we had the same doctor, so I spent that whole evening with my doctor. He teased me about having my appointment bright and early that next Friday morning.

Friday at 9 am my husband and son go with me to our thirty-five-week ultrasound appointment. The doctor brought in a student doctor, and he was checking for the baby's heartbeat. He could not find one. My doctor took the device and started to look then he said, "let's go to the ultrasound room to look." We got there and he showed me the baby and said, "there she is, but no heartbeat", he started crying.

Grace

I was confused and said what do you mean? He proceeded to tell us "I am sorry, but she is gone". Those words still ring in my head. The feeling of having a carpet pulled from under you is the only way to explain this feeling. He left the room and we all stood there like what in the world do we do now? We had a moment to cry and make phone calls. I called my mom who was visiting her friends in Minnesota, and she could not believe the news. Nothing prepared any of us for this.

The test was now how do I react to God answering our prayers but in His own way? We went through all the stages of grief, while making our way to the hospital to push out a baby who cannot stay with us. The only way we overcame this test was only by His grace. I tell you this was the hardest trial, but during it I could feel the prayers carrying me through moment by moment. This trial has strengthened my faith so much that I know Jeremiah 29:11 is still true for my life.

> *For I know the thoughts that I think toward you, saith the* Lord, *thoughts of peace, and not of evil, to give you an expected end.*

I would not do anything differently. I hope my children know that tough times will come, but in those moments, God wants to carry us. Trust in the Lord and lean not on your own understanding, in all your ways acknowledge Him. He will make your path straight.

For anyone who is experiencing a loss of a child, I know it does not feel right to bury a child you carried but know that God is still good. He gives and takes away, so we must still say blessed be the name of the Lord. God has restored me tenfold. I rejoice now because despite having one ovary, I am a mother of five children (four boys and a baby girl in God's presence). We continue to trust God with each child. The scripture I will leave you with is.

And ye now therefore have sorrow: but I will see you again, and your heart shall rejoice, and your joy no man taketh from you. John 16:22

Be Kind

Please be kind to others that may not look like you. You have no idea the battle people are facing, and your words can harm or heal. I have a passion for children who are on the autism spectrum. I provide therapy to them, and I feel called to this field. I intercede and stand in the gap believing God for His healing touch over these children.

To God be the glory, I am restored. I may not look like the next girl, but I am me and I am loved. The Lord formed me this way. These days I do not hide behind my prosthetic ear. I use my condition as an opportunity to teach my children. No matter how we look, we are all made in God's image!

Chapter Four
Time is Precious

Amarachi is my beautiful sister. Her resilience remains, despite what she has been through. She is always the life of the party and has a contagious laugh. I admire her joy and approach to life. You are beautiful inside and out. Her favorite line is "Every day is Mother's Day!" Indeed it is, you are an amazing mother!

Time

There is an endless wealth of information all around us. With the time we have it is unfortunate that more of us do not learn new skills. Time is a precious gift. What is influencing you? Be honest with yourself. This can dictate how your time is spent. When you take inventory of your spending, as I have previously stated, only then will you begin to see what your priorities are. Nowadays, time is mainly spent on social media.

What legacy are you building? In your absence, what kind of person would people say that you are? We live in a world where everyone has an opinion. Ladies keep it classy and watch the words of your mouth. In a social media age, where we speak before we think, this concept has been lost.

> *Be not rash with thy mouth, and let not thine heart be hasty to utter any thing before God: for God is in heaven, and thou upon earth: therefore let thy words be few. Ecclesiastes 5:2*

We can transform our lives by simply thinking before we speak. Most of us speak out of our emotions, but they are fleeting and change from moment to moment. How often have we regretted something we posted seconds after. Regrettably even if we change our mind and delete the post, it will forever be there. Ask yourself if the things you see on social media are uplifting or depressing. A majority of what you see online is usually not real. This is worth mentioning again. Photoshop and the age of AI is quickly changing our viewpoint on what reality is.

The Reality

We have our beautiful young girls and women selling themselves on Instagram, and platforms like only fans. All of this has an impact on the future. We need to begin thinking before we speak and act. The way you present yourself online and real-life matters. This information is forever, even after deleting posts, it is permanent. Only fans and pornography are harmful to both men and women. It desensitizes and objectifies both sexes. It exploits those involved and harms the mind. Our souls become entangled and tied to others. This creates soul ties and bondage. It is damaging to the soul. Hookup culture is weakening our society. When we choose to do things our own way, it leads to dysfunction and chaos.

> *But I say unto you, That whosoever looketh on a woman to lust after her hath committed adultery with her already in his heart. Matthew 5:28*

We have become immodest as a society and things are quickly unraveling. That is why I emphasized modesty. We can point the finger and blame only men, but ladies let's focus on the role we

play. We all play a part. How often have you scrolled and seen bikini shots, skintight gym clothes, suggestive poses? Ladies, we can do better than this. We are not for sell and are in fact selling ourselves short. The point is, we are in control of what we post. Post with wisdom and with the mindset that one day your children or grandchildren might see these pictures. Beyond that God sees it also. We are setting traps for men. That is why it's called a 'thirst-trap'. You will be accountable for the snares you lay.
Instead of endlessly scrolling try out a new hobby. Try hiking, gardening, poetry, or even kayaking. Get creative! You were made in the image of a creative God. He put that same creativity into all of us. This is the first book I have ever written, and I am amazed at the process. It took lots of time, but I enjoyed every minute. Fun fact, English is my second language, and I am always learning new words. The Lord helped me find the right words to write.

Spending time with God has helped cultivate things that were dormant in my life. Not having social media frees up time for creativity. At times I get bored and must think outside of the box. In that creative space wonders take place.

Account

The time we waste is a huge deal and taking accountability will hopefully help. I have been there my sister, scrolling and looking at reels that are an illusion and feeling down about myself. Take back your time and future. Think about the gifts and talents that God has given you. Make a habit of being still and present throughout the day. We all have the same amount of time. Start taking account of how you spend your time.

The most sobering thought is standing before God and giving account of how I spent my time here on earth. I ponder this often and frequently reflect on my time management, to ensure I am making effective use of the time He has given me here on earth. I want every purpose and plan that God has for my life to be fulfilled. The devil comes to steal, kill, and destroy. He steals our time by keeping us distracted. One of the most precious things we have on earth is the gift of time. The Bottomline is, the things we waste time on are pointless. I used to spend five hours or more daily on social media.

Follower

Social media has become an addiction for most women. To be set free might require prayer and fasting, as with any addiction. After deleting my accounts, I remember thinking, what do I do with the extra time I have? I was bored and felt alone at first. It took years to move forward and not look back.

No more invites or seeing what everyone was up to. No more notifications, and the occasional online interaction with my "friends." I soon realized most of my online friends were not real-life friends. No one really noticed I was gone. This was a hard pill to swallow, but I was honest with myself. This was the first time I sat down and really learned who my real friends were.

Take your time, (no pun intended) and if you fail get back up. We follow people that lead us to destruction. If they aren't pointing you to God, be careful. Try and set a daily timer or unfollow people that cause you anxiety. Life is meant for so much more and there are real connections the Lord would have us make.

Everyone is trying to be the next social media star or influencer. Don't be a follower, be a leader and be led by Jesus. Plain and simple. He is the best influence, and reading His Word is one of the best uses of your time. Spending time with Him has opened doors of blessings like never before. He is always waiting patiently for us to quiet our minds and seek Him.

Tribe

Going back to the importance of community, we need face-to-face connections with each other. We should strive to establish relationships that keep us accountable and help us grow. Recently I went to an event and stepped out of my comfort zone, introducing myself to a couple of ladies. I asked them if we could get in touch and meet up from time to time. In an anti-social society that sounds bizarre. Frankly, most of us are terrified at the thought of meeting new people.

Sisters sometimes life requires stepping out of your comfort zone. We can do all things through Christ who gives us strength. Always remember that. Without social media, I do things the old-fashioned way. It feels good to walk in that boldness and with God's direction I can make lasting new connections.

Start tracking how much time you spend on social media and reading the word of God. When you spend time mindfully, and with intention, fulfillment follows. I would recommend reading the book of Proverbs in its entirety. it is full of wisdom.

My tribe helped make this book happen. I was available to answer God's call and obeyed him. I spend quality time with the women God has gifted me with. We laugh, cry, and enjoy life together. It is a beautiful community, and I am so grateful. I have learned so much about life through the lens of these women. When I spend time with them it is quality: no phones, no scrolling. It is face to face; quality time spent together. They pray for me and uplift me. I now know who my faithful friends are. They are loyal and I love them. They have been there through every season of life.

We are communal beings and thrive when together. Our culture highlights introversion and being 'anti-social'. Sadly we are coined as the loneliest generation. Meaning people are dying from loneliness and lack of community. We need human interaction; it is a part of our makeup. Social media creates the illusion of community. It has become toxic to young minds globally. Depression, suicide, and anxiety have been on the rise since the inception of social media. Please know your limit and guard your heart and mind. The creation story emphasized the beauty of togetherness. God's design is always best, because He is the Creator and knows what we need.

> *And the LORD God said, It is not good that the man should be alone; I will make him an help meet for him.*
> *Genesis 2:18*
>
> *Two are better than one; because they have a good reward for their labour. Ecclesiastes 4:9*

Scripture Meditation

Ecclesiastes 3:1-8
To every thing there is a season, and a time to every purpose under the heaven: A time to be born, and a time to die; a time to plant, and a time to pluck up that which is planted; A time to kill, and a time to heal; a time to break down, and a time to build up; A time to weep, and a time to laugh; a time to mourn, and a time to dance; A time to cast away stones, and a time to gather stones together; a time to embrace, and a time to refrain from embracing; A time to get, and a time to lose; a time to keep, and a time to cast away; A time to rend, and a time to sew; a time to keep silence, and a time to speak; A time to love, and a time to hate; a time of war, and a time of peace.

Ephesians 5:16
Redeeming the time, because the days are evil.

Proverbs 13:3
He that keepeth his mouth keepeth his life: but he that openeth wide his lips shall have destruction.

Proverbs 18:21
Death and life are in the power of the tongue: and they that love it shall eat the fruit thereof.

Ephesians 4:29
Let no corrupt communication proceed out of your mouth, but that which is good to the use of edifying, that it may minister grace unto the hearers.

Matthew 12:37
But I say unto you, That every idle word that men shall speak, they shall give account thereof in the day of judgment. For by thy words thou shalt be justified, and by thy words thou shalt be condemned.

Matthew 15:11
Not that which goeth into the mouth defileth a man; but that which cometh out of the mouth, this defileth a man.

Proverbs 10:19
In the multitude of words there wanteth not sin: but he that refraineth his lips is wise.

Psalm 31:15
My times are in thy hand: deliver me from the hand of mine enemies, and from them that persecute me.

Romans 14:12
So then every one of us shall give account of himself to God.

Colossians 4:6
Let your speech be always with grace, seasoned with salt, that ye may know how ye ought to answer every man.

1 Corinthians 7:29
But this I say, brethren, the time is short: it remaineth, that both they that have wives be as though they had none;

James 4:4
Ye adulterers and adulteresses, know ye not that the friendship of the world is enmity with God? whosoever therefore will be a friend of the world is the enemy of God.

Things To Ponder

What do I wish I had more time to do?

How many hours do I average a day on social media?

How much time do I spend with God?

Am I pleased with my time management?

Who has the power to influence me?

Who is a part of my tribe and why?

In what ways do I waste time?

Prayer

Lord forgive me for speaking lies, hateful things or anything that was not right to say. Please help me to think before I speak. I pray to have the discernment to speak in love and to speak life over those around me.

Forgive me for being angry or speaking in wrath. Lord any word that was spoken over me that was not from you, please heal and remove it from my soul and spirit. Wash my mouth and place your words over me.

Please give me the strength to use my time wisely. I want more of you, and to be less distracted. In Jesus name. Amen!

Shadia's Testimony

Teen Mom

I met my boyfriend when I was fifteen, we started dating when I was sixteen, and by seventeen I was pregnant. All my friends at the time were getting pregnant. It was like a little assemble line. Some of the girls had "miscellaneous miscarriage" (a quiet abortion), others chose adoption. I was in the group that had and raised them. When you get pregnant as a teenager, you have three life altering choices to make. Adoption, abortion, or motherhood. None of those choices are easy. I chose to have my baby.

I was in love, and head over heels. We had walks in the park, and talked about everything. The beginning was innocent. When my mom found out we were dating, she opposed our relationship from the beginning. She hated his guts, and my mom cautioned me several times. She knew he was bad news. Unfortunately, I was strong willed and headstrong. I did not listen, and frankly I was too naïve to see what she saw.

Family

My mom and dad were teen parents also. This was a generational pattern. They divorced when I was eleven, and my family life at this time was unstable and in recovery mode. We were in and out of the courts. I felt like collateral damage and did not feel protected.

I was the oldest of four and therefore thought I knew a lot. My childhood was filled with trauma, and I was in survival mode constantly. Although I had a caring family, we lacked foundation and structure. I was a sweet and lovable girl, being raised by a single mom. My dad was not around much, and my environment made me grow up fast. I was independent, helped pay bills, and figured I was an adult. My mom was a cool mom.

I thought I knew everything about being a woman. My exposure to certain things made me think I was mature. The truth is I was so naïve at this time and paid the price dearly. After finding out I was pregnant, everything went downhill from there.

Love is Blind

One day my boyfriend and I were driving, and a random car was speeding up behind us. A truck full of girls were shouting at me. He told me to "pull over and just lock the door." I had no clue what was going on. It was during this confrontation that I found out; another girl was pregnant by my boyfriend. She was crying, upset, and trying to attack me in her anger. I could not believe what was going on. My fairytale love was built on dishonesty and betrayal.

After giving birth, I spent the night in the hospital all alone. The night my baby girl and I came home, he was on his way to a nightclub. The writing was on the wall. It was all bad, and I couldn't believe this was my reality. Also, when I was eight months pregnant, I found my baby daddy cheating on me at a barbeque. We never recovered from this typical baby mama drama. He kept having different children with other women. We were not on the same page, and I had to move on. Now I am a single mom.

Over the years, I hustled and provided for my daughter and me. I took her everywhere; she was my roll baby. I spent years picking up the pieces and figuring out my life. I supported her and I and kept it moving, and never looked back.

Special Needs

A lifetime goes by, and we moved to a new city. I meet a new man and things are going well. After dating for ten years, we married. Now it is time to have a baby and to my surprise I was struggling to conceive. I remember crying and saying, "I can't believe I wasted my womb." The most precious thing I felt I had. Now finally married to the man that I prayed for and can't give him a child. The irony of it all. It was now time to see a 'specialist.'

I was told by a Fertility Specialist that I had low ovarian reserve, and my best bet was to be a donor. I changed doctors and got a second opinion. I began fertility treatments. The purpose of the hormone injections was to help grow the egg. Shortly after the first round, I went in for my appointment and was told that the eggs had busted. I was devastated! What do I do now?

I declined to pursue more treatments and trusted God. It was too much to go through and I gave up. I got pregnant six months later and miscarried. That was my first miscarriage, and it brought my spirit down and stole my joy. I lost hope in having a baby.

Finally

I finally got pregnant again. Throughout the pregnancy, I was cautious and held my breath. I was considered high risk but no issues at all, it was a healthy pregnancy. I had another baby girl (my girls are twenty-two years apart).

She was sweet as a rose, strong and healthy. But at four months old things took a scary turn. She started having issues. It began with severe acid reflux and other symptoms. Later to find out, they were misdiagnosed seizures. She rapidly declined over the span of months. She was not hitting the developmental milestones and was not getting better with prescribed acid reflux medication. We were in and out of hospitals. After spending a week at the hospital, the doctors finally diagnosed her. Her seizures were reasonably managed.

There have been many moments where we did not think she would make it. During this trial I did not have time to be upset with God. I was grasping and crying out to God for dear life. I needed Him more than ever. My husband and I held our breath every single night for years. Her seizures were so bad and kept us in a state of PTSD. We were confused, desperate and felt like we were drowning. It was traumatic because for a while they had no idea how to treat her.

The only thing that brought my baby comfort was breast feeding. I breast fed her for many years. There were moments when she would seize while breastfeeding. Her teeth would lock up on me and I would just cry in pain while holding her, to comfort her.

They diagnosed her with Autism. She is getting the therapies she needs, and her seizures are better managed. Thank God! Developmentally she is behind but catching up. We have a great church family, and support system. I am so grateful for the people who have rallied behind us during this difficult season of our lives.

Teen Moms

To my fellow teen moms, read your Word to hear what God is saying to you. He will provide for your needs. Baby mama drama is not worth it. Sometimes the reality is we are one of many women that are being strung along. Also know that in your deepest despair cry out to God. I read the book of Matthews a million times, and it got me through my hardest storms. It is a long road, hang in there. Your child needs you. You will get through whatever comes your way.

Special Needs Mom

To have a child with specials needs is not the end of the world. It is a new direction, and you will be okay. There are many resources. Behavioral therapy, herbs, diet modifications etc. God is still best at doing what He does. When you are in deep despair, you surrender, and you let go. Let God guide you. That is when God does His best work. The doctors do not know, the medicines are not perfect, only God knows.

Chapter Five
Build Your Legacy

Shadia is one of the strongest women I know. She is selfless and constantly thinking of others. I am grateful for her constant example of humility and love. Keep going, you got this! I remember that day in the hospital when the baby girl made her arrival. She was holding her neck that first day and I marveled at her strength! She is a fighter and will overcome. May you see her generations of children. The best is yet to come!

The Future

Children are the future. This is not a cliché; it is the truth. How we raise them and what we pass on to them matters. Our children need us. Not social media, toys, or gadgets; just us. They need our time and attention. The attention we provide them builds their self-esteem and self-worth. There are countless people in this world void of the love and attention they needed as children. We can change that, one child at a time. This is not just for 'mothers'. This includes teachers, aunties, grandmas, god-mothers and anyone who has influence over them. Our viewpoints on children must change.

Families are the foundation of a society, and children are the future. They need to be loved, nurtured, and protected by both men and women. Animals are treated with more respect in our society, which is a shame. We are created in the image and likeness of God.

Lo, children are an heritage of the LORD: and the fruit of the womb is his reward. Psalm 127:3

Generational dysfunction can be an obstacle in this task of raising children with love. It can seem hopeless when our examples have been negative, but I encourage you not to feel defeated if this is you. Learn and continue to grow in this area. Your sons are priceless, and your daughters are not your competition. They are gifts from the Lord. Let us break these generational strongholds of neglect, and instead nurture the treasures God has blessed us with. We are all children of God. He is watching how we treat ourselves, and how we treat and care for our children.

Dig deep and learn about raising children. Research what sacrifices are involved and the realities of motherhood. Nine months of pregnancy is no small feat; it is not for the weak. I can tell you that from experience. It was both the most joyful and demanding thing I have ever done. During all three of my pregnancies I lost ten pounds, in the first trimester, from vomiting multiple times a day. I am sorry for this detail, but it happens. This is not how every pregnancy goes, so please have no fear! Some women have the opposite experience and feel great the entire time. It is a sacrifice, but well worth it. When you meet your child after nine months, nothing can describe the feeling of joy, every single time. It Is amazing and so rewarding. Our bodies are perfectly designed for the task.

Conception

In our culture abortions and the debate about children is a hot topic. We argue about when conception begins. Every soul has worth and is valuable. We all started as a period on a page and blossomed into the beautiful creatures we are today. The lord can redeem us even if we were "mistakes". We were never a mistake to him. Children are a blessing!

We all began this journey as children and are still children in the eyes of the Lord. We need to honor and respect the beauty of the children God has blessed us with. Choose life and wait on the Lord. Lean to him and not your own understanding. With each child that a woman brings into this world there is power and potential.

Doctors, lawyers, inventors of remarkable things, soldiers, plumbers, and potential fathers and mothers have been aborted in the womb of a woman. Their fate and destiny denied. They have no voice, so I speak for them. The womb is a sacred place. Yet it has become one of the most dangerous places for babies. *Over sixty-three million babies have been aborted in America alone and counting, according to a google search**. To actualize this number, the population size of France is sixty-four million according to *Worldometer.com*. That is an entire country, gone.

I speak on their behalf because their lives mattered, and they had no say in the matter. If this is you, I am not judging you. Please hear my heart. I am speaking life over you and want to tell you that your baby matters. It is never an easy choice to abort a child, but ladies let's try to do better. Every pregnancy in the womb is a living soul that God created. Only He can take or give life.

Voices

In the bible, people sacrificed their children to a pagan god named Molech. They did this in exchange for blessings, and prosperity. This was very evil in the sight of the Lord. He would bring swift judgement upon a land that shed innocent blood. When human blood is unjustly shed, it cries out to God. Yes, you read that correctly. Blood has a voice because it belongs to a living soul. The bible is clear that the life of every living thing, is in its blood. Can you imagine what sixty-three million babies crying out to God sounds like!? We need to repent as a nation.

> *And he said, what hast thou done? the voice of thy brother's blood crieth unto me from the ground.*
> *Genesis 4:10*
>
> *And shed innocent blood, even the blood of their sons and of their daughters, whom they sacrificed unto the idols of Canaan: and the land was polluted with blood.*
> *Psalm 106:38*
>
> *For it is the life of all flesh; the blood of it is for the life thereof: therefore I said unto the children of Israel, Ye shall eat the blood of no manner of flesh: for the life of all flesh is the blood thereof: whosoever eateth it shall be cut off.*
> *Leviticus 17:14*

And thou shalt not let any of thy seed pass through the fire to Molech, neither shalt thou profane the name of thy God: I am the LORD. Leviticus 18:21

The Womb

Being a mom is difficult, but the joys exceed the difficulties believe me. God is waiting with open arms to forgive you and cleanse you of the guilt and shame if you have had an abortion. If this is your story, Jesus's blood can cleanse you of your sins. That is why He died. There is no sin too great. His blood that was shed on earth, speaks forgiveness over our sins. He lived a blameless life and was a sacrifice to redeem us from the curse of sin. Maybe you have heard it before; God so love the world that He gave his only begotten son. His innocent blood being shed gave us life because life is in the blood. That is why His blood is precious and powerful!

> *How much more shall the blood of Christ, who through the eternal Spirit offered himself without spot to God, purge your conscience from dead works to serve the living God? Hebrews 9:14*

> *And to Jesus the mediator of the new covenant, and to the blood of sprinkling, that speaketh better things than that of Abel. Hebrews 12:24*

My heart goes out to any woman that has made this decision. And if you are facing this even now, I pray you cry out to God and allow His blood to cover you. I am praying and interceding on your behalf. Trust God with all your decisions and he will order your steps. Before conception, the Lord has a plan over your womb. The enemy has taken this heritage away from too many women. I want to proclaim that your womb is powerful, and the Lord is bringing forth greatness through our wombs. Have peace in knowing that he can forgive all our wrongs and restore our hearts. The path you choose matters. A generation that knows the worth of the womb is arising and casting down all lies that the enemy has told us. We build and not tear down. And that starts with our babies. The truth will set us all free if we uphold and accept it.

We Have Purpose

The next hot topic often debated is overpopulation. There are billions of people on earth, why have more children? Let me address this not as an expert, but with a little research. The information is available online to check. For instance, Japan is on the brink of chaos due to their women not having children. They are one of many nations facing this same crisis. Some nations are even offering financial incentives to have more children, due to the decline in numbers. The elderly outweigh the number of young people in some countries. If something is not done, we could lose a whole generation.

Financially I know having children can be expensive. There are ways however, you can offset the cost. We share and pass down clothes in my community. Children a lot of times do not need much. In fact, they play with household items rather than the fancy toys we purchase them. My children are deeply loved, and cared for and have been such a blessing to me. For the mamas facing infertility I pray you receive your blessing.

Practical Steps

Play the role God has given you. Ask him daily to supply your needs and quiet your fears surrounding children. It is the greatest task we have been given, to raise and steward the next generation. It requires humility, patience, and wisdom. Ladies, let us not walk in deception during this hour.

The mothers of Moses and Jesus were both faced with almost losing their children. Can you imagine if they said, 'my body, my choice'? Instead they chose to say, not my child. Your child is full of destiny and purpose. Your baby might be the next Moses this generation needs. Or perhaps a deliverer to lead the captives to the promised land. Your womb is precious, build your legacy. Know that your baby matters and has a purpose. Ladies, all our children are here for a reason.

Here are some practical things you can do before becoming a mother; be a nanny, work with children or volunteer for a field trip. Being a babysitter really helped equip me for this season of life. Experience helps to teach us different perspectives we might not already have. Check out some child rearing books and resources at the library. If you can be a foster parent that is great too. If you have nieces and nephews, volunteer to help with them on occasion. Trust me, their parents will be grateful.

The journey of motherhood comes with no manual or instructions. Raising children requires learning new things. You do your best and some days are not perfect. For all the mamas out there, you got this and are doing an excellent job! Be kind to yourself even on your bad days. We all have them. If you are overwhelmed, ask for help.

To all the mamas, you are amazing. The mamas waiting for the fruit of the womb, may you receive double for your trouble! Homeschool mamas, may God give you the patience to instruct your children. To the working mamas, may God strengthen you every single day. Mamas that adopted their children, God bless you. To the mamas who gave up their children via adoption, or have estranged children, God sees you and knows what you are going through. To the single mamas, keep your head up and stay strong. To the teen moms and older mamas may God fill you with joy. Whatever your journey to motherhood and building your legacy looks like, keep going.

Scripture Meditation

Psalm 127:4
As arrows are in the hand of a mighty man; so are children of the youth.

Matthew 19:14
But Jesus said, Suffer little children, and forbid them not, to come unto me: for of such is the kingdom of heaven.

Romans 8:16
The Spirit itself beareth witness with our spirit, that we are the children of God:

1 John 3:1
Behold, what manner of love the Father hath bestowed upon us, that we should be called the sons of God: therefore the world knoweth us not, because it knew him not.

Psalm 78:6
That the generation to come might know them, even the children which should be born; who should arise and declare them to their children:

Psalm 139:13-18
For thou hast possessed my reins: thou hast covered me in my mother's womb. I will praise thee; for I am fearfully and wonderfully made: marvellous are thy works; and that my soul knoweth right well. My substance was not hid from thee, when I was made in secret, and curiously wrought in the lowest parts of the earth. Thine eyes did see my substance, yet being unperfect;

and in thy book all my members were written, which in continuance were fashioned, when as yet there was none of them. How precious also are thy thoughts unto me, O God! how great is the sum of them! If I should count them, they are more in number than the sand: when I awake, I am still with thee.

Genesis 25:23
And the LORD said unto her, Two nations are in thy womb, and two manner of people shall be separated from thy bowels; and the one people shall be stronger than the other people; and the elder shall serve the younger.

Ephesians 1:7
In whom we have redemption through his blood, the forgiveness of sins, according to the riches of his grace;

1 Peter 1:19
But with the precious blood of Christ, as of a lamb without blemish and without spot:

Romans 5:9
Much more then, being now justified by his blood, we shall be saved from wrath through him.

Luke 1:41
And it came to pass, that, when Elisabeth heard the salutation of Mary, the babe leaped in her womb; and Elisabeth was filled with the Holy Ghost:

Psalm 22:10
I was cast upon thee from the womb: thou art my God from my mother's belly.

Things To Ponder

What have I done that feels unforgivable?

Do I trust God?

What are my viewpoints on children?

What areas need transformation in my heart and mind?

How was I raised and nurtured as a child?

Have I healed from my past hurts?

What kind of mother or women do I hope to be?

What guilt do I dwell on?

Prayer

Lord renew my heart and mind concerning children. Please forgive me if I have taken away a child's precious life. Whether through coercion, promotion, paying for or aiding an abortion please forgive me. Please silence the voice of any blood that is crying out against me.

I repent for choosing my plans over yours and ask that you would please shine your light and guide my way. Please give me the strength I need every day. Not my will, but your will be done in my life. In Jesus name. Amen!

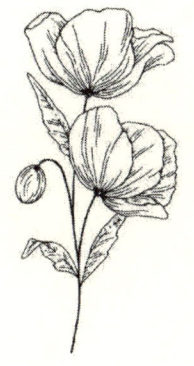

Sasha's Testimony

To My Baby

At twenty years old, I was faced with the hardest decision of my life. I found myself staring down at a little white stick with the word "pregnant". We were not ready for a baby, but being young and naive I hoped the man I loved would rise to the occasion. He was five years older than me and an accomplished officer in the Air Force. "We can't have this baby", he told me as he waved his gun around with the smell of whiskey on his breath. An empty bottle of Jack Daniel's sat next to him on his nightstand. "You need to get an abortion. I'm not ready and if you don't, I will kill myself" he said.

In hysterics, I realized I was forced to choose between two lives. The one growing inside of me or his. For weeks I looked to those around me for help. What choice was I to make? The lies of Satan infiltrated my mind through the mouths of people I called family and friends. "You are too young. He is right, you're not ready. You are going to ruin your life, it's only a shell. How will you support this child?" I wish I never listened to those voices. Influence is a powerful tool of the enemy, and he got exactly what he wanted.

November 11th, 2010 is the day I took my baby's life. Regret and pain burned so deeply into my heart. The morning of my appointment I downed sleeping pills to numb my inner cries. I was looking for one person to tell me not to do this. It never happened. As I waited for my name to be called, I felt like I was in the Holocaust going into the gas chamber. One by one I watched women enter the room with life in their womb, and one by one I saw them leave with a piece of their soul torn out.

I laid on the cold sterile table, being touched by hands that shed innocent blood. This was another day in the office for them and another check to collect. I opened my legs as they inserted a long tube and turned on the suction. The horrific sound of the machine still plays in my mind. The pain was indescribable as the doctor tore my baby apart and ripped everything out of me. I cried and yelled, gripping the nurse's hand tightly. Within moments, it was done. They quickly cleaned up and left me alone with blood dripping down my legs. I was numb and in shock.

What just happened? The reality of what took place did not hit me until I got home. Alone and unsupported, I dropped to my knees screaming. "Please, please I'm so sorry please give me my baby back, I just want my baby back!" I was begging God for another chance as I held my empty womb.

My boyfriend cheated on me the weekend after. I was abandoned, left to pick up the pieces alone. Doors to the enemy were opened. In the years following I was riddled with anxiety, anger, promiscuity, guilt, and shame.

Alcohol

Alcohol quickly became my best friend. It made me feel confident and liberated from my emotional anguish. I was looking in all the wrong places to fill a void. I was angry and wanted to get back at the world. I thought if men could do it, I could do it too. One drink became two, two became three and before you knew it, I was waking up with a man in bed that I met from the night before. This became my new normal. My dependency on alcohol grew and grew.

It affected my relationships and friendships. I put myself in dangerous situations time and time again. I didn't realize I had a problem. I was self-destructing, masking the pain over and over. Nothing could mask the pain. I grew anxious and combative while drunk. I got into ugly fist fights and would wake up with regret. In the mornings, when I sobered up, I would go on an apology train.

Despite my troubles I fell in love and married my now husband. We traveled the world together. We were happy but my past was still clinging onto me. We welcomed our first daughter shortly after. When she was eighteen months, alcohol became a point of contention in my marriage. For the first time I am hearing that I have a problem. My husband called me out and gave me an ultimatum. I needed help and wanted to fight for my marriage.

My Recovery

I knew I couldn't do it alone, so I started leaning on my faith. I held on to the promises of God, and He blessed me with back-to-back pregnancies. I could not drink therefore I learned to cope without alcohol, and to trust in God. Having my children is the greatest earthly love I have ever experienced. Becoming a mother made me want to be better. Honestly, my husband and children saved my life.

When I look at my children, I am reminded of what I took away. The guilt remains but I am slowly healing. God is starting to weave my story of redemption. God started to unharden my heart to the things that no longer served me. I started to see myself the way He sees me. My desire to live for the Lord outweighed my desire to satisfy my flesh. Sometimes the temptation to drink is still there, but I am learning to stay strong.

I had an abortion, but I am now forgiven. Through repentance and deep sorrow, God is restoring my heart. God picked some of the most broken people for His glory. I cling to these stories in the bible for hope, and it helps my healing process. It says that He works all things out for His purpose, and I know my pain has a purpose.

> And we know that all things work together for good to them that love God, to them who are the called according to his purpose. Romans 8:28

Advice

Although we are forgiven of our sins, it still comes with consequences. We live in a broken world. If you are like me and feel like you have no support to keep your baby, God will make a way for you. Look to Him to sustain you during this time. Do not be afraid. This road might come with challenges, but your true reward is in heaven. The world says it's your body and your choice, but the Word of God says different. When you are faced with a serious problem, look to God in prayer. Trust Him for the solutions, and He will not fail you.

> *For God gave us a spirit not of fear but power and love and self-control. 2 Timothy 1:7*

The company you keep is so important, surround yourself with God fearing friends. It can determine the outcome of your life. I pray that I can be that one voice to tell you. Your child matters! Choose life.

Chapter Six
Influence

The first time Sasha and I hung out, we went to sushi, and she told me her story. I was moved to tears, and we cried together while I listened to her grieve for her baby. I was humbled and saddened by her remorse. Her heart is so kind. We have been through thick and thin, and I am grateful for our friendship. Thank you for sharing your story, this took so much courage. You are not just a friend; you are my sister and I love you.

Comparison

Birds of a feather flock together. Who are your friends on social media and in real life? Choose your friends wisely and give your time to those that value you. Are your friends a positive or negative influence? This all affects the person you become. Women are the most susceptible to the power of advertising and influence.

I remember one day sitting in front of a computer for over five hours looking at the best of everyone's lives. I felt empty and I could not compete. Vacations, new homes, designer bags, highlight reels; I felt left out disillusioned and frankly depressed. I realized scrolling endlessly was to my peril. The reality is I was comparing myself to other people's lives, which is always a mistake. I deleted my Facebook page years ago and have never looked back. I tried Instagram for a month, a couple years ago, and those same feelings of inadequacy started to creep in. So guess what, I deleted it! This seems extreme and harsh, but in a society where anxiety is rapidly increasing it becomes a necessity.

Peace

Peace has become a priority in my life, and I protect it at all costs. Most look for peace in the wrong places, and cope with destructive habits. Maybe your friend is a substance, alcohol, marijuana, or pills/drugs. Perhaps it is binge eating, anorexia, impulsive shopping, or even pornography. You name your vice. These things can lead to self-destruction. We all need to look in the mirror and be honest and one by one address these negative influences. Can you function without these so-called friends? If you find that you can no longer function without some of these things you may be bound and need to be set free.

It is easy to see a drug addict and judge them, but all these things create bondages and lead to darkness also. Sometimes the worst decisions we make in life are while under the influence of a substance. In our society we like to blame it on "the alcohol," but ladies we need to be accountable of the kind of friends we make and keep. If you entertain such things, it has become an acquaintance. Let it go.

> *Wine is a mocker, strong drink is raging: and whosoever is deceived thereby is not wise. Proverbs 20:1*

Environment

Change your environment and the places that remind you of things that have been a struggle for you. They lead to destruction and can be detrimental. It is worth mentioning again, that I found freedom in Jesus! My addiction to marijuana was broken instantly, and it did not take years or months. The holy spirit gave me the strength every single day to say no. The choice was mine. Some days were harder than others but my desire to live for Christ was and is greater.

Find trusted friends and praying friends that have your best interest in mind. We become who we follow, and it is important to be careful who we align our lives with. Many women are jealous and compete with one another. This is not life building, nor is it fruitful. Traits such as jealousy and envy lead to contention and strife.

I am truly blessed to have wonderful friends that uplift me and want the best for me. I have had my share of negative influences and guard against them. Community is important for us as women. We need the support of one another. Good friendships can be a godsend. Ladies, there are good women that will help you fulfill your destiny and others that can derail your destiny. Choose wisely.

Spiritual Warfare

If you are addicted to a substance, please get the help you need before it is too late. Some addictions require fasting, praying and meditating on God's word. Substance abuse at times can be rooted in spiritual warfare. Fighting these things carnally can be pointless. Meet with trusted counselors and loved ones to determine what course of action is needed for your freedom. It is important to be honest with a trusted friend, because in silence substance abuse can worsen. Accountability is also vital. When someone knows what you are going through, they are better able to check on you or simply pray for you. It can be embarrassing to admit an addiction, but in secrecy it can spiral out of control. I have been there and taking those first steps are crucial.

I changed my environment and severed contact with those that tempted me into my previous lifestyle. I also changed the kind of music I listened to, immersing myself in God's word and worship music. It took me a while to make this adjustment because I was used to a certain type of music. I still practice these things and mainly listen to uplifting music. Secular music reminds me of who I used to be, and I guard against it because I want to stay free. Staying free does not happen by accident, it takes intention and small positive choices each day.

Start Today

Think about it, if you are trying to heal from fornication or the spirit of lust, the last thing you need is listening to sensual music. The lyrics paint a picture and are filled with suggestive thoughts. The same applies if you have bitterness or hatred. Heavy rock and hip hop might not help soften your stoney heart. These lyrics become chants and before you know it, you are becoming those lyrics. Music is powerful and influences us. Certain sounds and music can bring back memories, whether good or bad.

> *Wherein in time past ye walked according to the course of this world, according to the prince of the power of the air, the spirit that now worketh in the children of disobedience: Ephesians 2:2*

After changing my style of dressing, music that encouraged me to be a 'baddie' was no longer an option or helpful to me. I removed all reminders of things that kept me bound and in a destructive mindset. I must continually choose to be free and not go back. I remember the struggles I had and will always choose my restoration.

Through God we can overcome the battles we face. If you do not have the financial help to pursue healing, there is hope. Honestly, I could not afford professional help or even a counselor when I was going through my addiction and grieving my daughter's death. I solely relied on God. I had no other choice. Everyone is different and I want to encourage you to find the path that works for you.

Start today, it is not too late, you can do anything you put your mind to. May the Lord lead you to the resources you need. The lord is your best friend and comforter during times of great need. If you don't have any friends take heart you have a friend in Jesus. There are times we face loneliness even when others are around us. During this time run to Jesus, not a substance. A substance will only mask the pain temporarily. It will never heal the root issues. The root issues are what I encourage you to unmask and dig into. Healing from trauma, abuse and other heavy experiences can seem impossible. Just remember, with Jesus all things are possible.

Do not give up until you have found the peace you are looking for. Peace is priceless and a worthy goal for us all. When these issues are confronted, we transform and cope better with other trials that may come our way. Once these chains break, we change the trajectory of our future generations. Rewriting the rest of our stories is possible.

Scripture Meditation

John 15:13-15
Greater love hath no man than this, that a man lay down his life for his friends. Ye are my friends, if ye do whatsoever I command you. Henceforth I call you not servants; for the servant knoweth not what his lord doeth: but I have called you friends; for all things that I have heard of my Father I have made known unto you.

Psalm 1:1-3
Blessed is the man that walketh not in the counsel of the ungodly, nor standeth in the way of sinners, nor sitteth in the seat of the scornful. But his delight is in the law of the LORD; and in his law doth he meditate day and night. And he shall be like a tree planted by the rivers of water, that bringeth forth his fruit in his season; his leaf also shall not wither; and whatsoever he doeth shall prosper.

1 Corinthians 15:33
Be not deceived: evil communications corrupt good manners.

Proverbs 13:20
He that walketh with wise men shall be wise: but a companion of fools shall be destroyed.

Proverbs 18:24
A man that hath friends must shew himself friendly: and there is a friend that sticketh closer than a brother.

Proverbs 27:6
Faithful are the wounds of a friend; but the kisses of an enemy are deceitful.

James 3:16
For where envying and strife is, there is confusion and every evil work.

John 14:27
Peace I leave with you, my peace I give unto you: not as the world giveth, give I unto you. Let not your heart be troubled, neither let it be afraid.

Proverbs 31:4-9
It is not for kings, O Lemuel, it is not for kings to drink wine; nor for princes strong drink: Lest they drink, and forget the law, and pervert the judgment of any of the afflicted. Give strong drink unto him that is ready to perish, and wine unto those that be of heavy hearts. Let him drink, and forget his poverty, and remember his misery no more. Open thy mouth for the dumb in the cause of all such as are appointed to destruction. Open thy mouth, judge righteously, and plead the cause of the poor and needy.

Ephesians 5:18-19
And be not drunk with wine, wherein is excess; but be filled with the Spirit; Speaking to yourselves in psalms and hymns and spiritual songs, singing and making melody in your heart to the Lord; Giving thanks always for all things unto God and the Father in the name of our Lord Jesus Christ;

Things To Ponder

Who are my best friends and why?

Have these friends brought me closer or further from God?

What positive things have they brought into my life?

Will these friends be around when trials come?

What negative habits do I have that need to be broken?

What places or things should I avoid, to grow in this area?

Would I go to a women's bible study in my area? If not, why?

Prayer

Thank you for the good friends you have given me. Lord help me to be kind and loving towards the people you have placed in my life. If there is anybody that is in my life that you have not ordained to be in my life, please remove them.

Father, give me discernment to know the spirit of those around me. Any harm, evil or danger that is being devised against me please destroy those plans. Father guide my friendships and relationships. In any area of addiction that I am bound, Lord I pray for your healing and restoration in my life. Please bring your light into every darkness of my soul.

I will take this moment and pray for you if unhealed trauma is part of your story.

Father, I pray for my beautiful sister and ask that you cleanse the open wounds and the sorrow within her heart. Please Lord, cover these women that are shattered with a peace beyond understanding. Please clothe your daughters with joy and with peace. Give them the consolation and clarity they need to heal. Lord for every woman that is chained to dysfunction through a traumatic experience I pray for full restoration over their lives. Break every chain Jesus! You can do all things and I pray that your healing touch would come upon their lives even now. Father, please heal the wounds of molestation, heal the pain of rape, and please mend the broken hearts of those that are victims of incest. Do a new thing in every woman's life that is reading this prayer. In Jesus name I pray. Amen!

Janique's Testimony

Plan B

My plan was to take a plan B first thing in the morning. July 2011, I had unprotected sex. Before this I was celibate for years and had been waiting on God. I got impatient and had a moment of weakness. My plan was to go to nursing school, and having a baby was not part of my plan. I found myself in a situation and I had a choice to make.

The night before my plan of taking plan B, I had an encounter that changed my life. As I thought about my plan and how I was going to take care of my 'mistake', God spoke. He told me clear as day that it was a baby and gave me a name for the child. When he said the name, the voice thundered and echoed. The room quaked and I was terrified and scared! Keep in mind at this point I didn't even know if I was pregnant, let alone the sex of the baby.

All I knew was that I had made a 'mistake' and needed to fix it by taking a plan B. I started to do research on when life begins in the womb. I decided again that I would still take plan B. At this stage it was harmless, so I thought. A voice again boomed and said, "it's a baby!" I ignored this voice but immediately heard it louder and with more power! I could not shake this and decided I would not take plan B and see what happens.

Baby Boy

Weeks later sure enough I was pregnant. Dad and I were not on the same page at all. Nine long months later, I had a baby boy and became a single mom. Financially and emotionally, I had to raise this child on my own. Being a single mother has not been easy, but God has always provided. After my son's birth my career path changed. I was now in early childcare (unlicensed in-home childcare provider). I also became a foster parent during this time. My walk with God deepened and I learned to rely on him for my daily needs. I was waiting for his timing yet again.

In 2016, my mother passed, a week before Mother's Day. My life was rocked! It was surreal and unbelievable. However, her words of encouragement and her love for me kept me going. At this time in my life, I drew closer to God than ever before. He told me to be bigger, and I had no clue what He meant by that.

I learned to be the bigger person and started to see the bigger picture of every situation. Over the years, I continued to wait on God and got weary in the waiting process. To be honest I was upset at God. Here I am waiting all these years, raising this child by myself, working, struggling and mentally in a fog. I felt frustrated and discouraged.

Sacrifice

When I became a mother, I denied myself of the 'pleasures' of life. I stopped drinking, smoking, and partying overnight. All the sacrifices I had to make while watching others live their lives felt so unfair. My baby's father went on with life as usual while I took care of our son. I had to learn to forgive and let go of my plans and be a mother. Most nights and days were with my child, and I had no break.

Here I am again walking out my faith every day and celibate, while waiting for my husband. On top of this, I gained a lot of weight due to years of depression. Eighty plus pounds to be exact! This was uncomfortable and I didn't even know who I was. I was hurting and crying out for help.

Finally, God sent me support and good friends to help take my mind off my situation. God also showed me that I needed forgiveness and showed me the bitterness, unforgiveness and hatred I had in my heart. For years I had unforgiveness for my child's father. God told me that He already forgave him, and I needed to do the same.

Repeat

Ten years later in 2021 I found myself in the same situation yet again. I felt defeated, and reached another point of frustration. I had another slip up. If you have ever been celibate some of you know what I mean. I took a pregnancy test, and it was positive. I had a choice to make again, would I take plan B or not? I was so close to making this choice and could not believe I was pregnant again.

This was the first time in years I slipped up and I even used a condom. To my surprise, the condom was removed without my consent. I was tricked by the baby's father and so angry at myself. During this time, I remembered my encounter with God and what He said. I knew that an abortion was not an option.

I decided to follow through with the pregnancy. I had no choice but to see this through. I did not want blood on my hands. Mentally I was distraught. Here I was a Christian girl who got exposed fornicating and the truth came to light. I felt guilty, ashamed, and devastated. I got tired of doing it God's way and paid dearly for my impatience. Here I am going through this again with another man, another child and alone again.

During the pregnancy God gave me a name also. I had a strength I've never had while pregnant. During winter (Christmas time) I caught covid while pregnant, losing twenty pounds in a week! I had no idea it was covid, and still worked while sick. I managed to cook for Christmas and take care of my son while pregnant. God really kept me because I shouldn't have made it. According to the experts. I am African American, overweight, have underlying health issues, and was pregnant.

Another Boy

Three months later my baby boy arrives via C-section. He was breached, and his cord was around his neck. It was a miracle he was alive and healthy. The doctor mentioned while sewing me up that I was not supposed to make it off the table; it was an emergency c-section. They did not have time to put me under. It was a miracle, we made it out alive.

Before his arrival I was putting together plans to operate a family childcare business. I was focused and driven to get this done. By God's grace I received my business license, six days before I gave birth. God's timing couldn't have been better. This is huge, because I grew up in the projects of Brooklyn, New York, on Government assistance.

Forgiveness

In my life I have always had a plan B. I grew up in a dog-eat-dog world. So, trust was not an option. I was always in survival mode and a backup plan was a must. This was driven by fear. In life I have done this with just about everything. Growing up in the projects shaped my identity and was part of my make up. I grew up with that mindset and didn't realize how it affected my relationship with God and other people.

The root of my problem was trust. This was a poverty mindset that had to go, and I am working towards this. It is a generational stronghold I have had to confront and rebuke! I'm learning to fully trust the Lord and let go of my plans and be led by Him in all things. I'm learning how to stay out of my own way, really letting go and letting God.

Along the way I forgave this child's father as well and realized I had to take accountability for the part I played. I was not supposed to be having sex at all. The lessons God taught me from my first child's father really helped me with this situation. I didn't hurt like before and I was able to move forward quickly. Through these years I have taken losses and things have happened to me.

I love the story of Joseph in the bible. He kept going and kept his integrity through his problems. Things haven't always been fair in my life and when I have had the chance to repay evil for evil, I have chosen to repay good.

After my mother's death, I started to see the bigger picture and God showed me a new perspective. Jospeh knew the bigger picture. He forgave his siblings and Potipher's wife for their betrayals also. He always chose to be the bigger person. In life people will mistreat you. Keep your integrity and keep your mind on the palace.

The tables have turned in my favor, and God worked it out for my good. I am currently a successful business owner, and debt free. I have two paid vehicles and paid off $50,000 worth of debt. Praise God! Now I am breaking away from Government assistance.

Single Moms

I had weight loss surgery in 2023 and I am currently 116 pounds down. I feel better and getting my life back. As an adult I am learning new things about myself. God has restored me, and I am still being restored. On the outside looking in, people judge me for being a Christian single mom of two children from two different fathers, and not married.

I had to learn that people don't have a heaven or hell to put me in. Only God has the final say. In the book of John, a woman was caught in adultery and the men wanted to stone her. Jesus said, "let him without sin cast the first stone." No one cast a stone. This is when I realized no one could judge me. Those people wanting to stone her/condemn her represented feelings like guilt, and shame. It is my repentance, my relationship with God, and what He says that matters to me.

For the single moms, God will still use you. Your value does not change, because of what you went through. God still sees you as his beautiful daughter. No matter the drugs, the partners, or the secrets you keep to yourself, He can still use you. At the cross He died to forgive every single sin. While on the cross, He was being spat at, accused, hurt, and still chose to die and forgive us. God is so good, even to the death of His only son.

To the single moms, repent and keep it moving. Stop doubting God and stop doubting yourself. Don't let guilt and shame hold you back. Have grace and mercy on yourself, and don't allow people to condemn you. Don't limit yourself nor look for outside approval. You are of great worth and have value. Don't let a man put value on you and stop trying to prove yourself to others. Pick up your cross and walk.

As a mom I worried that my sons' ten-year age gap would affect their bond/relationship. To God be the glory my son wrote this:

My Little Bro Jacob
In the heart of a town, where sunlight gleams,
Lived Judah and his brother, bound by dreams.
Hand in hand, through fields of green,
Their laughter echoed, a joyful scene.

Judah, strong and wise, with eyes so bright,
Guided his brother through the day and night.
With every step, he led the way,
Teaching, protecting, come what may.

His brother, young and full of glee,
Looked up to Judah, his mentor, you see.
Together they played, in fields of gold,
Their bond a treasure, forever told.

Through storm and calm, they stood as one,
In the dance of life, beneath the sun.

*With each passing day, their love grew strong,
A melody of brotherhood, an everlasting song.*

*So here's to Judah and his little brother,
In each other's arms, they find no other.
Bound by blood, by love they're tied,
In their journey together, side by side.*

Chapter Seven
Speak Life

I have known Janique since high school. I have watched this woman blossom into a warrior of Christ before my eyes. Our friendship has kept me accountable and has encouraged me. We grew up together and started as girls and now mighty women of God! You are loyal and have always been one call away. Thank you for the beautiful years of friendship and loving me. In faith I declare, your name is about to change, Mrs.! I love you. Iron sharpens iron.

Words

The words we speak have power. In Genesis, through words, the entire creation was made. He said it and it happened. He also gave us the power to speak. We form our lives through thoughts and words. Speaking carelessly without thought has consequences.

> *And God said, Let there be light: and there was light. Genesis 1:3*

There was a time when I used to speak with no filter. Before getting married I thought, and always said, "there are no good men left". One day God checked me and told me to speak life over that area of my life. This sparked a journey of choosing my words carefully. That year I started to proclaim that there was a good man out there for me. I started to slowly believe it and met my husband later in that same year. You see, if I did not align my tongue with truth and life I would continue to expect a negative outcome.

Our society has made speaking recklessly normal. We live for the drama, but why has that become the norm? The woman I am today is a direct outcome of my thoughts, words, and actions. I choose what enters my mind, heart, soul, and spirit. This seems deep but really everything we are begins with a thought.

If every day I stare in the mirror and tell myself I'm ugly, over time it will become truth to me. Instead, I tell myself I am created in the image of God, and I am perfect the way he made me. When thoughts of anxiety and chaos try to enter, meditate on the source of peace and light. Admittedly, these intrusive and negative thoughts come often but I counter them with God's word. His words transform me from the inside out. Take inventory of your thoughts and start building life in your mind. One of my favorite Proverb says.

> *Death and life are in the power of the tongue: and they that love it shall eat the fruit thereof. Proverbs 18: 21*

He gives us peace that surpasses all understanding. Even in the middle of the storms of life, you may find that you are weak. Start proclaiming that you are strong, and God will make a way. There are countless studies that show when people get sick or ill, their attitude will determine their capacity to recover. Meaning if a person is negative, they quickly decline in health. In contrast the ones that believe they will make it usually have a higher probability of recovery.

Suggestions

Start taking inventory of what steals your peace. There are many things that can disturb our minds. Such as the news, social media, hearing bad news about people dying, or watching murder mysteries. If these thoughts go unchecked it can open negative spiritual doors.

> *But those things which proceed out of the mouth come forth from the heart; and they defile the man. For out of the heart proceed evil thoughts, murders, adulteries, fornications, thefts, false witness, blasphemies: These are the things which defile a man: but to eat with unwashen hands defileth not a man. Matthew 15:18-20*

Speaking life giving words is a game changer and has really opened doors of blessings in my life. Give it a try. When you are tempted to speak negatively towards someone or a situation, I encourage you to say something positive instead. With time your attitude might change.

Some suggestions to help you speak life; include reading the Bible, sing edifying songs, talking with God, experiencing time in nature in silence. Also reach out to friends that speak with grace. If you find yourself surrounded with negativity this might be a challenge. So begin to check your thoughts each day.

> *Finally, brethren, whatsoever things are true, whatsoever things are honest, whatsoever things are just, whatsoever things are pure, whatsoever things are lovely, whatsoever things are of good report; if there be any virtue, and if there be any praise, think on these things. Philippians 4:8*

Thoughts

What you think and say about yourself matters. Your words have the power to build or destroy. Take the time to speak kindly to those around you. If they matter to you, let them know. Kindness is such a beautiful art. If you have said something hurtful (we all have at some point), try to consider how the recipient feels and apologize if possible. I was called tomboy, not by choice, and it almost shaped my identity.

I'm grateful that God had more in store for my life. You see, I accepted what others thought of me, rather than what I was created to be. Which is a woman. I was a woman then and still a woman now. I grew into my body and am grateful for the growth I have experienced since that season of life. So please be mindful how you speak to others, it matters a great deal.

When you change how you speak, your thoughts will begin changing also. Purity of mind brings peace. Speaking life giving words has changed my life. I dwell on the wonderful things God is doing in this generation. It's popular to focus on the wrong, but there are many good things happening simultaneously. May the blessings of the God of Abraham, Isaac and Jacob fill your heart and mind with joy. May He give you peace in your storm and overwhelm you with his love and comfort. May every word not spoken in kindness over you be uprooted from your heart. The pain, the hurt and the betrayals washed away. May you find your identity and seek your Heavenly Father. He loves you and cares deeply for your soul.

I love you and hope that you are blessed and receive healing over your soul, body, and spirit. You are a temple and when you begin to view yourself from that perspective things change. Your thoughts about you mature and blossom into beautiful things. A temple is beautiful, holy, clean, and pure. May your vessel be cleansed and overflowing with the rivers of life. You are blessed in His image, speak life ladies.

Scripture Meditation

James 3:5-11
Even so the tongue is a little member, and boasteth great things. Behold, how great a matter a little fire kindleth! And the tongue is a fire, a world of iniquity: so is the tongue among our members, that it defileth the whole body, and setteth on fire the course of nature; and it is set on fire of hell. For every kind of beasts, and of birds, and of serpents, and of things in the sea, is tamed, and hath been tamed of mankind: But the tongue can no man tame; it is an unruly evil, full of deadly poison. Therewith bless we God, even the Father; and therewith curse we men, which are made after the similitude of God. Out of the same mouth proceedeth blessing and cursing. My brethren, these things ought not so to be. Doth a fountain send forth at the same place sweet water and bitter?

2 Corinthians 10:3-5
For though we walk in the flesh, we do not war after the flesh: (For the weapons of our warfare are not carnal, but mighty through God to the pulling down of strong holds;) Casting down imaginations, and every high thing that exalteth itself against the knowledge of God, and bringing into captivity every thought to the obedience of Christ;

Colossians 3:2
Set your affection on things above, not on things on the earth.

Psalm 139:23
Search me, O God, and know my heart: try me, and know my thoughts:

Isaiah 26:3
Thou wilt keep him in perfect peace, whose mind is stayed on thee: because he trusteth in thee.

Luke 6:45
A good man out of the good treasure of his heart bringeth forth that which is good; and an evil man out of the evil treasure of his heart bringeth forth that which is evil: for of the abundance of the heart his mouth speaketh.

Romans 8:6
For to be carnally minded is death; but to be spiritually minded is life and peace.

Proverbs 4:23-27
Keep thy heart with all diligence; for out of it are the issues of life. Put away from thee a froward mouth, and perverse lips put far from thee. Let thine eyes look right on, and let thine eyelids look straight before thee. Ponder the path of thy feet, and let all thy ways be established. Turn not to the right hand nor to the left: remove thy foot from evil.

James 1:26
If any man among you seem to be religious, and bridleth not his tongue, but deceiveth his own heart, this man's religion is vain.

Proverbs 15:26
The thoughts of the wicked are an abomination to the Lord: but the words of the pure are pleasant words.

Things To Ponder

What do I think about myself?

Are these things true or lies?

Who told me these things about myself. Where did they stem from?

Am I mostly negative or positive?

How can I improve or speak more life-giving words?

What area of my life needs a complete change of attitude?

Write proclamations over your life. (Example- I am courageous, strong, I can do anything etc.)

Prayer

Lord, please help me to speak your will over my life. Direct my tongue and use my mouth to bless and not curse. Forgive me for speaking in anger or with a foul mouth. Help me to tame my tongue every single day. I need you and at times it is not easy to speak life.

Fill me with your words of truth and wisdom. Help me to navigate and see the best in myself and others. I can do all things through you and believe that each day I will learn to speak with intention and grace. In Jesus name I pray, Amen!

Chibudom's Testimony

Waiting

I might be a Guinness world record holder. In the span of eight years, I attended thirty-three weddings and have been a bridesmaid in eight of them. No, I am not a wedding planner. Every couple of months, like clockwork, I would get a wedding invitation. I would purchase a dress for each wedding and travel to celebrate.

During this season of life, I was single, a virgin and waiting on God. Dating as a virgin was a challenge. Most men were scared or simply just wanted to have fun and not commit. There were long periods where I would avoid dating. For years it felt like I was passed up, overlooked, and forgotten about. I shared in the joys of my friends finding their husbands, but sadly I always wondered when my time would come.

Here's a little context about myself. At the age of sixteen, I was sent to a different state to live with my brother. In a new environment, and having to navigate life without my mom or dad, I had to grow up fast.

My dad died when I was just four years old. On top of that, my mom and I did not understand each other. Losing the love of her life, she was left with six little faces to remind her of what she lost. I can't imagine the pain she went through. I'm the youngest of six and her focus was rightfully elsewhere.

Change

After my dad died, I had a couple of different stepdads. With each new stepdad came a new set of rules. It was exhausting and as a child I did not know how to process all these changes. I always longed for a dad, but these new dads were not my dad and could never replace him. In addition, watching my mom's various relationships affected my standard of what I thought a man should be; let alone what a husband looked like.

Each stepdad illuminated a different marriage dynamic; it was hard to keep track. This was difficult and created friction between my mom and I. Step siblings and the changes that come with a blended family were overwhelming. If you know, you know. I attended twelve different schools before graduating high school.

The stepdads and divorces forced environmental changes. This continued to grow my resistance and further complicated my mom and I's relationship. At times I was rebellious and unsure of how to communicate. I will mention that I had a Christian upbringing so that helped anchor me.

Glimpse of Hope

Fast forward, I graduated high school and went to college in Minnesota. I got my Bachelor of Arts in Nutrition. I met very nice people and worked hard to achieve the things I pursued. My career was thriving, but the untouched part of my life was the relationship department.

Throughout college I tried my hand at dating to no avail. The virginity topic always came up, and it was a make or break for most men. Sadly, they liked the thought of my virginity but once they realized I was serious about waiting for marriage, they were out! Usually within weeks of dating, as soon as they found out I was a virgin, the breakup was inevitable. They would always say they needed to see if we were compatible sexually or not.

Finally, I thought I found the one! He was the first man that didn't pressure me and seemingly respected me. Eventually things didn't last. The small respect made me blind to the other issues in our relationship at large. That was my first glimpse of hope and when we broke up, it shattered me. It was an eye-opening moment of realization; my standard of men was off.

Worth

My life experiences had formed my views and created deep insecurities. The death of my father and each stepdad created a wound. There was a lack of stability from men in my life that I deeply yearned for. I was trying to fill this void with a man and when that was taken, I felt lost. All my life I thought my worth came from marriage and from a man's approval. I believed that to feel safe required having a man.

To cope after the breakup, I sought medication for anxiety and depression. Hindsight looking back, I idolized the idea of marriage. I knew that God would bless me, but I placed the promise above God! I was weary if I'm honest and felt like God owed me a marriage because I was doing it His way. I wanted it in my timing and not His. I became self-righteous in my pursuit of marriage and hit rock bottom. I didn't feel like myself, post medication and post break up. I needed a change of scenery.

West Coast

I moved to Las Vegas and reunited with my sisters. It was a huge move, but I'm glad I took the leap of faith. I faced many obstacles in making this needed change. For instance, on the road to Vegas, I hit a deer and totaled my car; but that's a different story for another day! I made it safe and began a new life on the West coast. Did I mention, no more snow!? I lived with one of my sisters and we enjoyed some years of singleness together. The dating scene in Las Vegas was trash, I mean peculiar! There were times I wanted to completely give up.

This was the range, on a second date (not the first date), a man told me his family was a part of a globally recognized terrorist group. My mind was blown, no pun intended! I also went on a few dates with a man in a wheelchair and thought things were going well. During dinner, he looked me in my eyes and told me he thought I was "spunky" and wanted to be just friends. To say my self-esteem was rocked is putting it lightly. Not because he was in a wheelchair, but it was yet another man that rejected me, when I thought things were going well. You know the feeling ladies when you only make the friend zone. It can be awkward and frustrating! Online dating was not an option, it was not my style.

An Act of Faith

There were days where I was confused and asked God if He forgot about me. Everyone around me kept finding their prince charming and having babies. I felt like I was behind in life, but I kept on and continued to trust God.

In 2020 the world as we knew it, shut down. My hopes and dreams of marriage did as well. I mean where was I going to meet a man, with the shutdown? With not a lot to do, I took a road trip to Utah. While there I stumbled across a coffee shop and while sitting there, I spoke with a stranger.

It was a vulnerable time for me, and I shared with her about my dormant passions of being a bride. Funny enough, she was the owner of a bridal store and had the same name as my mother, Bridget. We went to her store, and she encouraged me to try on a dress. She also told me I was going to get married. I video timed my sister, and she told me to buy it. It sounded crazy but I felt the same.

This was my dream dress, and it gave me hope. I bought the dress in May 2020. At this point keep in mind that I don't have a man or any prospects at all. I was twenty-seven years old, single and a virgin. A leap of faith sometimes is all we need in life.

Later in the year I meet someone, and we begin dating! A year later, May 2021 my boyfriend told me he loved me, and in May 2022 we got married and I was a bride! I can't make this up. God showed up and restored the years I felt I lost waiting! It was not until after everything happened that God walked me through the significance of the date that I bought my dress in faith.

To Those Waiting

Your purity is important and beautiful. You are the bride of Christ and need to walk in that. Whether you are a virgin or not you are still a bride. Before my time came, every wedding I attended was a test of my heart. Would I be jealous, angry, or happy for my friends? The choice was mine. I chose to celebrate the women that went before my time. Naturally of course I did wonder if my turn would ever come. The lord looks at our hearts and will put us in situations to clean our hearts.

Younger me always felt that I was living in God's plan B "the backup plan"; when life looked a certain way and didn't go in the vision, I thought it would. In my waiting season I had to be honest about the parts of my life experience that marked me and needed his restoration. I became self-righteous while waiting and truly had to give God the hurt that was on my heart. Just because I was a virgin, did not make me better than the next girl. I was caught up in being pure as a transaction to be redeemed for a blessing.

Full transparency, I almost missed the bigger picture, the blessing in being obedient. Obedience to God isn't about receiving anything from Him, but His protection.

Singleness is not a curse; purity is your protection. I want to share my story to encourage and give hope to those that are waiting. Waiting for seven years was not easy! It took healing, pruning, getting delivered from medication and trusting God wholeheartedly.

Waiting for God can be a challenge, but the wait is well worth it. For the women waiting for their husbands my advice is to stay faithful and keep your eyes on God. Surround yourself with likeminded people and make sure to make strong boundaries during dating. Know what you are willing to do and not do. Compromise is not wise. Listen ladies, before I became a wife, I was already acting like a wife and dressed accordingly. I carried myself with respect and honor. Looking back, it truly is a miracle, and it was God that kept me all those years.

In my singleness He taught me the depths of purity. He protected me and helped me even when I was tempted to do what everyone else was doing. Be the difference in this world and go against the societal norms. There will always be something we have to wait for in life. Wait well and trust God. His plans are better than ours. My favorite scripture is Jeremiah 29:11.

Chapter Eight
New Beginnings

Chibudom is my little sister. I remember that face time call like it was yesterday. You looked like a beautiful bride. I knew that God would bless you, in His timing. You took a leap of faith and God honored that. You are a pillar for Christ, and your womb is blessed. Thank you for always thinking of me and caring for me. You are the best.

Glory

All glory and honor belong to the Almighty God. You have read of the glory of God in each of our lives. Despite our failures and shortcomings the glory of God shines in us. He restores and He forgives us of sin.

> *The definition of the word "Glory". Praise, honor, or distinction extended by common consent.*

Begin today, not later. Your heavenly father made you for great things and I am here to testify that He makes broken things beautiful. My name means God is beautiful and He truly is that. From my heart to yours, we overcome by our testimony. Our past is for another woman going through her struggle. Share with others about how God has healed and delivered you.

Your story matters and this is just the beginning. Maybe God is telling you to step out on faith. Perhaps to join a bible study group, or simply to bare it all and become who He created you to be. No more hiding behind masks, things, or identities that may not be the real or true you.

I hid my true self for years and was ashamed of my hair, lips, failures and so much more. This is my first time sharing my testimony of what I went through and my restoration journey. I am free to finally be me. It feels amazing to say I finally embrace who I am. You are much more than the labels that have been placed on you.

No one is beyond restoration and healing. This is not a quick fix nor a promise of change. I know what worked for me and I want to inspire and give hope. When my daughter died three days after her birth, I was broken and in a place of need. I cried out to God, and He delivered me. I learned the preciousness of life and the beauty of faith through my trial.

This has been a lifelong journey and there are still tough days. Life is not easy, but you are here for a purpose and a reason. Find out what the meaning and destiny for your life is. No one can undertake this task but you. Every day is a new day to start anew. If you failed yesterday get back up and try again.

May God Restore You

Stay strong in all that you encounter. You are stronger than you know. When we are weak then He is strong and perfecting you by His grace. Weakness draws us closer to God because it is then that we realize that we need help. May He be your anchor in the storms of life and guide you to green pastures and restore your soul. May the weight of His glory overshadow and bring forth His promises and plans over your life.

Remember, fear paralyzes, but faith releases. Choose faith to weather the storms and stay afloat. Keep your eyes fixed on Jesus. He is holding you even now. You have read our stories and can see that we are imperfect and at times broken.

When Jesus walked on earth, he was a carpenter. A carpenter builds. He is our spiritual carpenter and when you have Jesus, your foundation is secure and firm. He is our rock when we face adversities and trouble. You have read of His Glory and His power amid our storms. We lean on Him, and He holds us during times of difficulties.

Overcome

After every storm there is a rainbow. This is dedicated to all the babies we have lost, all the women that are widows and grieving the love of their lives, for the young girl who has no direction or clear path in her life. This is for the confused, abused and neglected.

Jesus makes all things new, cheers to your new beginning! We are praying for every girl that reads this book. Know that we are thinking about your story and how ours can help transform your life. Take one step at a time: baby steps.

In conclusion, I hope all these stories inspired you. These women have all helped me grow in one way or another. I thank and honor these beautiful women that have helped me on my journey. We tripped so that you can avoid some of our mistakes. Everything works out for our good. With all my love, Chiamaka.
May the Lord Restore Your Glory.

Baby Steps

In the loving memory of my baby girl, Tzipporah. Your life mattered, we only had three days, but it's okay. I think about you often. I am the woman I am because of you. The pain I went through was not in vain. Three days changed my life forever. I birthed you but was reborn myself. This is for you, baby girl. I am writing this on your behalf, you saved my life and I share your testimony as well. I am grateful and I love you. Until we meet again.

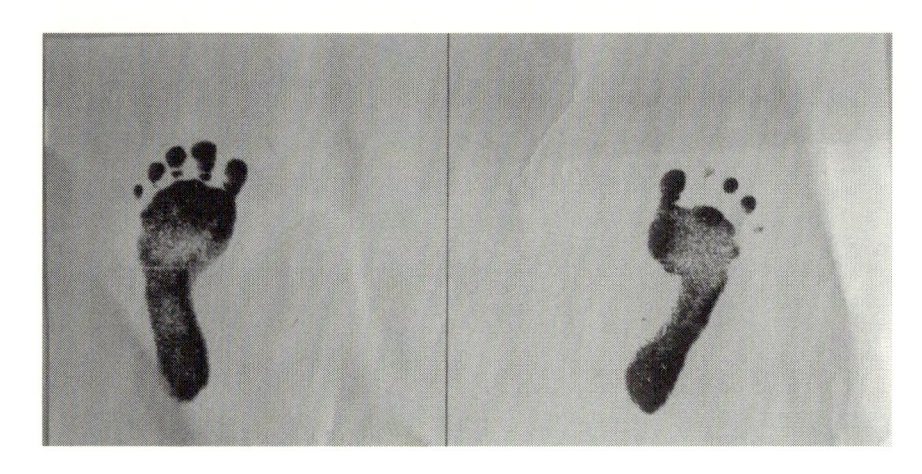

Closing Meditation

Psalm 3:3
But thou, O Lord, art a shield for me; my glory, and the lifter up of mine head.

Psalm 57:8
Awake up, my glory; awake, psaltery and harp: I myself will awake early.

Romans 8:18
For I reckon that the sufferings of this present time are not worthy to be compared with the glory which shall be revealed in us.

Romans 3:23
For all have sinned, and come short of the glory of God;

Habakkuk 2:14
For the earth shall be filled with the knowledge of the glory of the Lord, as the waters cover the sea.

2 Corinthians 3:18
But we all, with open face beholding as in a glass the glory of the Lord, are changed into the same image from glory to glory, even as by the Spirit of the Lord.

Isaiah 42:9
Behold, the former things are come to pass, and new things do I declare: before they spring forth I tell you of them.

Isaiah 43:1-2
*But now thus saith the L*ORD *that created thee, O Jacob, and he that formed thee, O Israel, Fear not: for I have redeemed thee, I have called thee by thy name; thou art mine. When thou passest through the waters, I will be with thee; and through the rivers, they shall not overflow thee: when thou walkest through the fire, thou shalt not be burned; neither shall the flame kindle upon thee.*

Joel 2:25-26
*And I will restore to you the years that the locust hath eaten, the cankerworm, and the caterpiller, and the palmerworm, my great army which I sent among you. And ye shall eat in plenty, and be satisfied, and praise the name of the L*ORD *your God, that hath dealt wondrously with you: and my people shall never be ashamed.*

John 1:14
And the Word was made flesh, and dwelt among us, (and we beheld his glory, the glory as of the only begotten of the Father,) full of grace and truth.

John 15:8-10
Herein is my Father glorified, that ye bear much fruit; so shall ye be my disciples. As the Father hath loved me, so have I loved you: continue ye in my love. If ye keep my commandments, ye shall abide in my love; even as I have kept my Father's commandments, and abide in his love.

Revelation 21:5
And he that sat upon the throne said, Behold, I make all things new. And he said unto me, Write: for these words are true and faithful.

References

"Restore." Merriam-Webster.com Dictionary, Merriam-Webster, https://www.merriam-webster.com/dictionary/restore. Accessed 25 May. 2024.

"Glory." Merriam-Webster.com Dictionary, Merriam-Webster, https://www.merriam-webster.com/dictionary/glory. Accessed 25 May. 2024.

Morris, K, Dorman, S. May 4, 2022. America saw more than 1,000,000 abortions each year between 1975 and 2012 Retrieved from Over 63 million abortions have occurred in the US since Roe v. Wade decision in 1973 | Fox News *

Worldometers.info. 26 May 2024 Dover, Delaware, Population by Country (2024) - Worldometer (worldometers.info) U.S.A.Worldometer.com

If any of these testimonies encouraged or helped you, please let us know. If you would like discipleship, have questions, or need resources, email us. We would love to hear from you.

Any further Inquiries/Bookings

Restorebookclub@gmail.com

Made in the USA
Columbia, SC
11 September 2024